The Cooking Experience

Revised Edition

by

Marion P. Thomas

© 1994   Experience Publishing Co.
P.O. Box 1153
Valley Center, CA 92082

Distributed by:
ElderSong Publications, Inc.
P.O. Box 74
Mt. Airy, MD 21771

Copyright © 1994 Experience Publishing Company
P. O. Box 1153
Valley Center, CA 92082
(760) 749-3141

Revised Edition March 1995
Second Printing June 1997

ISBN 0-9657291-3-3

Cover Photograph
by
S.W. POLITE & ASSOC.

INTRODUCTION

This cookbook has been compiled with recipes that are simple to prepare with common ingredients and readily available equipment. The recipes are ones that I have used in my ten years of working with older adults in convalescent or assisted care homes, but they can be used with any group where group participation or demonstration is the goal. That is how it got the name of THE COOKING EXPERIENCE.

Starting with basics, it is not necessary to use the kitchen as a meeting place. All of the recipes for Appetizers, Salads, Breads, Muffins, Main Dishes, and Desserts can be prepared in a room that is equipped with a table and an electrical outlet that can take the load of a small appliance without popping a circuit breaker.

Limitations in time and equipment are overcome in the recipes, created hands-on, over my last ten years. An imaginative cook can overcome many culinary obstacles. Since classes cannot go to the kitchen, the kitchen, consisting of a toaster oven, electric frying pan, or hot plate, plus utensils and ingredients goes to the class. Each recipe page includes a list of ingredients, equipment, and utensils to use from start to finish. In fact, before leaving home, I use the recipes as my check lists to make sure I am fully prepared.

At the start of my classes, I had to experiment with many recipes, some worked, others were a disaster, but I finally developed this file that works well. Originally I considered if the recipe could be prepared in a time frame of 1 hour 50 minutes class time, then I had to copy the recipe, think through each step of the recipe and make a list of equipment. Since baking in a toaster oven requires successive bakings per recipe, I had to plan for time for three bakings. Of course, a conventional oven requires less time because the recipe could be baked in one time period. Preparations and set up usually require 30 minutes. Clean up must be allotted for as well.

It is advisable to make a schedule and keep a record of the recipes used and the dates. Holiday specials are always included, even minor holidays: i.e. Chinese New Year and Cinco de Mayo. This plan is not written in stone, but can vary with sales found in the market or a request from a person or a group.

Usually only one complete recipe is prepared. This recipe normally would serve 8 to 10 people, but I just divide the product into portions for tasting for the whole group. Therefore the size of the sample varies according to the number served.

My purpose in compiling THE COOKING EXPERIENCE is to provide this information in a convenient format for you to use to instruct, stimulate, and entertain the group. Bon Appétit!

Marion P. Thomas

COOKING NOTES: When baking muffins or cupcakes in the toaster oven, mini muffin tins are very useful···the tins fit nicely into the oven, bake faster than the regular size and can produce 12 servings or stretched to 24 halves. Since one recipe usually yields 2 1/2 or 3 dozen muffins,successive bakings are required. I use three tins, sliding in one after another. Normally disposable aluminum loaf and oblong pans that fit into the oven are useful for some recipes and can be reused.

Clear glass mixing bowls make it easier for everyone to watch the preparation taking place···I try to arrange my ingredients and equipment on the table so as not to obscure the view. Using paper towels on the table as a work surface is my method of having a clean area anywhere. They are also useful for cleaning up at the conclusion of the class.

HELP: If you have any question or comments, please contact me at:
P. O. Box 1153
Valley Center, CA 92082
or call
760-749-3141

TABLE OF CONTENTS

APPETIZERS

CHEESE STICKS

1 stick of pie crust mix or 1/2 package of pie crust mix (follow the directions on the package)

1/2 cup shredded cheddar cheese   1/8 teaspoon mustard

1 teaspoon paprika

1. Place all ingredients in a ziplock bag(freezer strength). Be sure to follow the directions on the pie crust package as to the quantity of water.
2. Pass around and have the people squeeze the bag to mix well.
3. Roll on lightly floured waxed paper to 12"x8" rectangle.
4. Cut into strips 1/2" wide x 4" long.
5. Place on ungreased baking sheet.
6. Bake at 425°F for 10 to 12 minutes.

EQUIPMENT NEEDED

zip lock bag   oven

measuring cups   measuring spoons

rolling pin   waxed paper

knife   baking sheets

flour   spatula

pancake turner   paper towels

serving dish

CHICKEN PUFFS

2 Tablespoons margarine

2 cups finely chopped chicken

1/4 cup flour

1/4 cup chopped celery

1/2 teaspoon salt

2 Tablespoons pimiento

1 egg

2 Tablespoons white wine

1/4 cup shredded Swiss cheese

1/4 cup mayonnaise

1. Melt margarine in 1/4 cup boiling water.
2. Add flour and salt and mix until mixture forms a ball.
3. Remove from heat , cool slightly and add egg and beat vigorously.
4. Stir in cheese.
5. Drop dough on greased sheet using 1 level teaspoon for each puff.
6. Bake at 400°F for 20 minutes.
7. Remove cool and split.
8. Combine remaining ingredients and fill each puff with 2 teaspoons.

EQUIPMENT NEEDED

hot plate

oven

pan

measuring spoons

bowl

measuring cups

2 spoons

teaspoon

spatula

knife

cutting board

non-stick spray

paper towels

serving dish

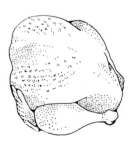

EMPANADITAS

2 cups flour

1 1/2 teaspoon baking powder

1 teaspoon salt

1/2 cup shortening

Relleno de Legumbres

1/3 cup cold water

1. Stir together flour, baking powder and salt.
2. Cut in shortening until particles resemble cornmeal.
3. Add water slowly to form ball. Divide into 20 balls.
4. On floured waxed paper, roll each ball into a 4" circle.
5. On greased baking sheet, place 1 Tablespoon filling into each. Moisten edges with water, fold in half, and press edge with fork to seal.
6. Brush top with milk.
7. Bake at 425°F for 15 to 18 minutes or until golden.

RELLENO DE LEGUMBRES

1 small zucchini

1 large tomato

2 oz. chopped green chilies

3/4 cup cheddar cheese

1. Trim ends from zucchini and cook in small amount of water 10 min.
2. Drain and chop.
3. Peel, seed, and chop tomato.
4. Combine all ingredients.

EQUIPMENT NEEDED

oven

measuring cups

2 spoons

fork

waxed paper

milk

baking sheet

knife

2 bowls

measuring spoons

pastry blender

rolling pin

pastry brush

non-stick spray

serving dish

paper towels

FRANK EGG ROLLS

3 franks, coarsely chopped

sweet and sour sauce

3/4 cup bean sprouts, chopped

8 egg roll wrappers

3/8 cup water chestnuts chopped

oil

1. In bowl, mix together franks, bean sprout, water chestnuts, and
   3 Tablespoons sweet and sour sauce.
2. Lay an egg roll wrapper out flat (keep others covered)
3. Evenly distribute 1/8 of frank mixture down the center of wrapper.
4. Brush edges with water.
5. Fold over filling and press together seam then pinch ends to seal.
6. Repeat with each wrapper.
7. Place seam down on greased or oiled baking sheet. Brush rolls lightly with oil.
8. Bake at 425°F 15 to 20 minutes - after 10 minutes turn rolls over.
9. Cut each roll with sharp knife into thirds.
10. Serve with sweet and sour sauce.

EQUIPMENT NEEDED

oven

bowl

cutting board

knife

measuring cups

measuring spoons

water

oil

pancake turner

baking sheet

serving dish

paper towels

FRANKFURTER KEBOBS

8 franks

pickled onions

bacon, cut into cubes

sweet pepper, cut into chunks

French Dressing

1/2 teaspoon salt

1/4 cup vinegar or lemon juice

3/4 cup oil

1/8 teaspoon pepper

1/4 teaspoon mustard

1. Cut each frank into four pieces.
2. Mix French Dressing and marinate franks for 30 minutes.
3. Preheat grill or electric frying pan.
4. Skewer franks alternately with bacon, onions, and pepper.
5. Grill or broil until browned, turning often.

EQUIPMENT NEEDED

knife

bowl

measuring spoons

skewers

paper towels

cutting board

measuring cups

spoon

serving dish

oven or barbeque grill

GUACAMOLE SPREAD

2 avocados

2 Tablespoons sour cream

1/8 teaspoon garlic powder

1/4 teaspoon salt

1 teaspoon lime juice

1/2 small onion, chopped

1 small tomato, chopped

1. Mash avocados.
2. Add sour cream, garlic powder, salt and lime juice.
3. Stir in onion and tomato and mix well.
4. Or put ingredients in zip lock bag and mix by passing around room.
5. Use as dip or spread.

FIESTA DIP

3 **GUACAMOLE SPREAD** recipes

3 tomatoes, chopped

1 cup shredded Monterey Jack cheese

Tortilla chips

ripe olives, chopped

2 cups cheddar cheese

Arrange on round platter, putting guacamole in center and decorating in wedges or concentric circle with the remaining ingredients.
Serve tortilla chips separately.

EQUIPMENT NEEDED

knife

measuring spoons

cutting board

serving bowls

2spoons

zip lock bag

table knife

2 bowls

tortilla chips

paper towels

HAM BISCUITS

1 1/4 cups flour   6 ounces chopped ham

1 Tablespoon baking powder   1/4 cup chopped green onion

1/2 teaspoon salt   1/2 cup parmesan cheese

1/4 lb. cold margarine   1/3 cup milk

2 teaspoons shortening   3 Tablespoons mayonnaise

3 Tablespoons prepared mustard

1. Mix flour, baking powder, and salt.

2. Add margarine and shortening, cut into coarse meal.

3. Add ham, onions, and cheese, then mix until blended.

4. Add milk and mix until dough holds together.

5. Shape into 1 inch balls on greased baking sheet.

6. Indent into the center of each ball (I used the handle of a wooden spoon).

7. Bake at 375°F for 10 minutes.

8. Remove from oven, indent again.

9. Bake 10 more minutes.

10. Mix mayonnaise and mustard and fill center of each ball.

11. Bake 3 to 5 minutes. Serve warm.

EQUIPMENT NEEDED

bowl   spoon

spatula   cutting board

knife   oven

non-stick spray   pancake turner

measuring cups   measuring spoons

sauce dish   serving dish

paper towels   pastry cutter

MEXICAN SEAFOOD TARTLETS

16 slices sandwich bread

3/8 cup melted margarine

Mexican Seafood Filling

paprika

FILLING

1 cup salad dressing

1/3 cup grated Parmesan cheese

1/3 cup shredded Swiss cheese

1/3 cup chopped onion

1/4 teaspoon Worcestershire sauce

2 drops hot sauce

2 oz. baby shrimp

2 oz. cooked crab meat, flaked

1. Preheat oven to 400°F.
2. Using a rolling pin, flatten slices of bread and cut 2 1/2 inch circles from each slice.
3. Dip into melted margarine, coating both sides.
4. Press into mini muffin tins. Bake 10 minutes or until golden brown.
5. Remove from oven and fill with prepared filling.
6. In medium bowl, combine all ingredients of filling except seafood. Mix until blended.
7. Stir in shrimp and crab meat.
8. Sprinkle tops with paprika.
9. Place under broiler until golden and bubbly.
10. Serve immediately.

EQUIPMENT NEEDED

2 bowls

measuring spoons

spatula

rolling pin

small container for melting margarine

serving dishes

measuring cups

wooden spoon

mini-muffin tins

cookie cutter

oven

paper towels

MINIATURE REUBENS

2 8 ounces package rye cocktail bread   mustard

1/2 pound sliced corned beef   8 ounces thin sliced Swiss cheese

8 ounces sauerkraut, drained   1/2 pound margarine

1. Spread half bread with mustard.
2. Top with folded corned beef to cover bread.
3. Spread 1 teaspoon sauerkraut on beef.
4. Place 2 thin slices of Swiss cheese to cover bread.
5. Top with remaining bread.
6. In electric frying pan, melt 4 Tablespoons margarine.
7. Sauté sandwiches (DO NOT CROWD).
8. When golden brown, turn and brown other side.
9. Cut and serve warm.

EQUIPMENT NEEDED

electric frying pan   knife

pancake turner   cutting board

small bowl   serving dish

paper towels

NACHOS AND QUESADILLAS

NACHOS

1 bag tortilla chips   1 cup shredded Monterey Jack cheese
1 4 ounce can chopped chili peppers

1. Spread chips in single layer on baking sheet.
2. Sprinkle with cheese and peppers.
3. Bake 5 minutes at 400°F.

QUESADILLAS

6 ounces Monterey Jack cheese   4 ounces chopped chili peppers
3/4 cup refried beans   12 6" tortillas

1. On each tortillas, spread cheese, peppers, and beans.
2. Fold in half, secure with a wooden pick.
3. Bake on baking sheet for 5 to 8 minutes or until cheese is melted at 400°F.

EQUIPMENT NEEDED

oven   measuring cups
baking sheet   baking dish
serving dish   pancake turner
knife   paper towels

ORIENTAL BEEF BALLS

1 pound ground beef

1 teaspoon salt

1/8 teaspoon black pepper

1/4 cup chopped onion

1 clove garlic, minced

2 Tablespoons cornstarch

1/4 cup water

1/2 cup celery sliced

1/2 cup carrot sliced

1/2 pound bean sprouts

1 teaspoon ginger

1 cup beef bouillon

1 Tablespoon soy sauce

1. Season meat with salt and pepper and shape into 1" balls.

2. Heat pan and brown meat balls a few at a time. Remove from pan.

3. Add onion and garlic and sauté until tender but not brown.

4. Add celery, carrots, and bean sprouts, cover and cook about 10 minutes or until tender.

5. Blend ginger, cornstarch, soy sauce, and water. Stir into vegetable mixture and cook until thickened.

6. Add meat balls and cook until heated through.

EQUIPMENT NEEDED

electric frying pan

knife

measuring cups

pancake turner

serving dish

cutting board

wooden spoon

measuring spoons

bowl

paper towels

PARMESAN CRESCENTS

3/4 cup margarine

1 pint cottage cheese
  (small curd)

1/8 teaspoon salt

2 cups flour

1 cup grated Parmesan cheese

1. Preheat oven to 400ºF.
2. Blend margarine, cottage cheese, and salt.
3. Add flour and mix until blended.
4. Divide into 4 or 6 balls.
5. Roll on floured waxed paper to 7" or 9" round.
6. Sprinkle with 2 Tablespoons cheese.
7. Cut into 8 wedges, roll from wide end and sprinkle with remaining cheese.
8. Bake 20 minutes and place on racks to cool.

EQUIPMENT NEEDED

oven

bowl

measuring cups

spatula

rolling pin

knife

baking sheet

paper towels

spoon

measuring spoons

waxed paper

serving tray

racks

PIZZA STICKS

1 can refrigerator breadsticks

24 thin slices pepperoni

2 Tablespoons Parmesan cheese

1/2 teaspoon Italian seasoning

1/4 teaspoon garlic powder

1/2 cup pizza sauce

1. Separate and unroll breadsticks.
2. Place 3 pepperoni slices in a row over 1/2 of breadstick.
3. Fold remaining half of breadstick over top, seal end and twist.
4. Place on ungreased baking sheet.
5. Combine cheese, seasoning, and garlic powder and sprinkle over each breadstick.
6. Bake at 350°F oven for 15 to 20 minutes. Cut into sections. Serve with pizza sauce.

CORN DOG TWISTS

1 can cornbread twists

8 hot dogs

1 Tablespoon melted magarine

1 Tablespoon Parmesan cheese

1. Unroll dough into 1 long sheet and seal center perforations.
2. Separate dough into 8 long strips.
3. Wrap each one around a hot dog.
4. Place on ungreased baking sheet with ends of dough tucked under the hot dog.
5. Brush with margarine and sprinkle with cheese.
6. Bake at 350°F for 12 to 16 minutes. Cut into sections and serve.

EQUIPMENT NEEDED

measuring cup

small bowl

baking sheets

serving dish

paper towels

measuring spoons

oven

pancake turner

knife

SAUSAGE ROLLS

8 precooked sausage links
water
1/2 cup margarine

2 cups flour
1/2 teaspoon salt
2 eggs

1. Preheat oven to 400ºF. Spray baking sheet with non-stick spray.
2. Cut margarine into flour and salt.
3. In 1 cup measure, beat eggs and add water to 2/3 cup.
4. Add 6 Tablespoons of egg mixture to flour mixture.
5. Roll out dough 1/2 inch thick on floured waxed paper and cut into 5 inch squares.
6. Brush with egg mixture
7. Roll sausage and seal ends.
8. Place seam side down on greased baking sheet.
9. Bake for 20 minutes or until golden brown. Cut into 4 pieces each.

EQUIPMENT NEEDED

oven
pastry blender
fork
waxed paper
baking sheets
serving dish

bowl
cup measure
rolling pin
knife
non-stick spray
paper towels

SEAFOOD TARTLETS

1 loaf thin sliced bread   paprika

6 Tablespoons margarine, melted

FILLING

1 cup mayonnaise   1/4 teaspoon Worcestershire

1/3 cup grated Parmesan cheese   sauce

1/3 cup shredded Swiss cheese   2 drops Tabasco sauce

1/3 cup chopped onion   4 ounces crab meat

1. Preheat oven to 400°F.
2. Flatten bread with rollilng pin and cut with 2 1/2" cookie cutter.
3. Dip into margarine and press in muffin tins.
4. Bake 10 minutes or until golden brown and cool in pans.
5. Fill each shell with filling mixture and sprinkle tops with paprika.
6. Broil until golden brown and bubbly.
7. Remove from pan and serve immediately.

EQUIPMENT NEEDED

oven   muffin tins

rolling pin   2 small bowls

measuring cups   measuring spoons

spoon   spatula

serving dish   knife

cutting board   cookie cutter

paper towels

SESAME SEED TURNOVERS

1 3 ounces package cream cheese

1/4 pound margarine

sesame seeds

1 cup flour

1 egg white, slightly beaten

SAVORY FILLING

2 eggs

2 cups shredded Muenster
    cheese (8 ounces)

1/4 teaspoon Tabasco sauce

1/8 tsp. salt

1 Tablespoon grated onion

1. Preheat oven to 375ºF.
2. Place cream cheese, margarine, and flour in a ziplock bag and mix.
3. Form in flat ball (refrigerate) and roll out on dough 1/8" thick on
    floured waxed paper. Cut into 2 1/2" rounds.
4. Place a teaspoon of filling on each round, fold, and seal with a fork.
5. Brush tops with egg white and sprinkle with sesame seeds.
6. Bake at 375°F for 20 to 25 minutes.

EQUIPMENT NEEDED

ziplock bag

measuring spoons

circle cutter

waxed paper

spatula

spoon

pastry brush

serving dish

measuring cup

grater

rolling pin

oven

small bowl

paper towels

fork

metal spatula

STUFFED MUSHROOM CAPS

3/4 pound medium mushrooms, cleaned and stems removed

8 ounces crab meat   8 ounces cream cheese

1/2 cup garlic croutons   Parmesan cheese

paprika

1. Preheat broiler and spray broiler pan with non-stick spray.
2. Mix together crab meat, cream cheese and croutons until mixture is blended. (This could be done by placing the ingredients in a ziplock bag and passing it around the group to be squeezed until mixed).
3. Mound mixture into mushroom caps.
4. Sprinkle tops generously with cheese and paprika.
5. Broil until piping hot and serve immediately.

EQUIPMENT NEEDED

bowl   ziplock bag

1/2 cup measure   measuring spoons

oven   serving dish

paper towels   non-stick spray

SWEDISH MEATBALLS

1 slice bread soaked in water

1 1/2 pounds chopped beef

2 eggs

1 Tablespoon margarine

1/4 cup chopped onion

3 Tablespoons chopped parsley

2 Tablespoons margarine

flour

1 1/4 teaspoons salt

1/4 teaspoon paprika

1/2 teaspoon grated lemon rind

1 teaspoon lemon juice

1/4 teaspoon nutmeg

1/8 teaspoon allspice

2 cups consommé

sherry (optional)

1. Beat eggs and add to meat.
2. Melt margarine and sauté onion in electric frying pan.
3. Add onion, wrung bread, parsley, spices, lemon rind and juice to meat and eggs.
4. Mix lightly with hands.
5. Shape into small balls and brown in margarine.
6. Drop into consommé and simmer 15 minutes in pot or add consommé to frying pan.
7. Remove meat and make gravy by adding 2 Tablespoons of margarine and 2 Tablespoons of flour for each cup of stock. Cook and stir until smooth, then season with sherry.
8. Reheat meatballs in gravy and serve.

EQUIPMENT NEEDED

2 bowls

hot plate

measuring spoons

cutting board

spatula

pot

electric frying pan

measuring cups

knife

wooden spoon

plate for bread

paper towels

SWEET AND SOUR MEATBALLS

3/4 pound ground beef or turkey

3 Tablespoons bread crumbs

1 teaspoon Worcestershire sauce

1/4 teaspoon salt

1/8 teaspoon pepper

1 egg white

8 ounces tomato sauce

1 1/2 teaspoons lemon juice

1/4 cup brown sugar

1/4 cup raisins

1/2 cup diced onion

1. Mix meat, crumbs, worcestershire sauce, salt, pepper, and egg white in large bowl.
2. Form into meatballs 1 inch in diameter.
3. Spray electric frying pan with non-stick spray, heat pan.
4. Add meatballs turning occasionally to brown on all sides.
5. After browning meatballs, add onion and toss so the onions cook without browning.
6. Add tomato sauce, lemon juice, brown sugar and raisins.
7. Simmer 15 minutes, add salt and pepper to taste. If necessary to increase sour, add more lemon juice.

EQUIPMENT NEEDED

electric frying pan

measuring cups

spoon

knife

serving bowl

non-stick spray

bowl

measuring spoons

spatula

cutting board

paper towels

SWISS AND FRANK SPIRALS

1 pound frankfurters

1 package refrigerated biscuits

2 Tablespoons sesame seeds

1 package process Swiss cheese slices

2 Tablespoons margarine, melted

1. Preheat oven to 400ºF and spray baking sheet with non-stick spray.
2. Cut franks into 4 pieces and slit.
3. Insert piece of cheese into each slit.
4. Quarter biscuits.
5. Wind biscuit in spiral fashion around franks.
6. Place on baking sheet and brush with margarine and sprinkle with sesame seeds.
7. Bake at 400°F for 10 minutes.

EQUIPMENT NEEDED

oven

measuring cup

cutting board

paper towels

non-stick spray

knife

brush

serving dish

baking sheets

TACO TARTLETS

TORTILLA CHIP FILLING

1/2 pint sour cream

2 Tablespoons taco sauce

2 ounces chopped ripe olives

3/4 cup coarsely crushed tortilla chips

TACO CRUST

1 pound lean ground beef

2 Tablespoons taco seasoning mix

2 Tablespoons ice water

1 cup shredded Cheddar cheese

1. Preheat oven to 425° F.
2. Prepare filling. Mix all ingredients in small bowl.
3. In larger bowl, mix beef, taco seasoning and ice water for crust.
4. Press beef into bottom and sides of mini muffin tins to form a shell.
5. Place spoonful of filling into each shell - mound slightly.
6. Sprinkle cheese over tops.
7. Bake 7 to 8 minutes.
8. Using the tip of a knife, remove tartlets and serve immediately.
9. Makes 30 appetizers.

EQUIPMENT NEEDED

oven

measuring cups

tablespoon

muffin tins

serving dish

two bowls

measuring spoons

knife

spatula

paper towels

21

TURKEY-SAUSAGE APPLE TRIANGLES

1 sweet apple (Cortland)

1 teaspoon lemon juice

1/2 teaspoon sugar

8 ounces Italian style turkey sausage, casings removed

1 teaspoon water

2 teaspoons prepared mustard

1 package frozen puff pastry, thawed

1 egg, lightly beaten

1. Preheat oven to 400°F.
2. Peel, core, and chop apple and toss together with lemon juice and sugar.
3. Crumble in sausage meat. Add mustard and mix well.
4. On lightly floured waxed paper, roll 1 pastry sheet at a time to 15" x12" rectangle.
5. Cut into 3" squares. Spoon a teaspoonful of filling onto each square and brush edge with egg mixture before folding into triangle.
6. Brush with egg mixture after sealing edges, but be careful not to brush cut edge of pastry.
7. Place on foil lined baking sheet.
8. Bake for 20 minutes or until golden and puffy.

EQUIPMENT NEEDED

bowl

cutting board

measuring spoons

spatula

waxed paper

teaspoon

baking sheets

oven

serving plate

knife

measuring cups

spoon

rolling pin

flour

pastry brush

aluminum foil

pancake turner

paper towels

VEGETABLE DIP

2 cups sour cream or cottage cheese, small curd

1 package dry vegetable soup mix   crackers or vegetables

1. Mix together in a bowl or place in freezer weight ziplock bag.
2. Use as a dip or spread with crackers or vegetables.

EQUIPMENT NEEDED

zip lock bag   spoon

serving dish   paper towels

knife   cutting board

FRESH SALSA

2 tomatoes, peeled and chopped	1 teaspoon oil
2 Tablespoons minced onion	1 teaspoon vinegar
3 Tablespoons canned chopped chiles	1/2 teaspoon salt
2 Tablespoons chopped cilantro(optional)	tortilla chips

1. Combine all ingredients, stirring well.
2. Place in a serving bowl. May be used with tortilla chips or vegetables.

EQUIPMENT NEEDED

measuring spoons   knife

cutting board   bowl

spoon   spatula

serving bowl   paper towels

VICKBURG CHEESE ROLL

3/4 cup Roquefort cheese

3/4 cup soft cream cheese

3/4 cup shredded cheddar cheese

paprika

1. Blend with a fork until smooth.
2. Roll into sausage shape or ball shape.
3. Sprinkle paprika on waxed paper and roll cheese in it until coated.
4. Chill and serve with crackers.

NUT CHEESE BALLS

1 cup Roquefort cheese

2 Tablespoons margarine

1 teaspoon paprika

1 cup cream cheese

1 teaspoon Worcestershire sauce

a few grains cayenne pepper

1. Mix all ingredients in a bowl and work into a paste.
2. Shape into 1 " balls.
3. Roll in chopped nuts or herbs such as chopped parsley.
4. Chill and serve.

EQUIPMENT NEEDED

bowls

fork

spoon

serving dish

waxed paper

measuring cups

measuring spoons

crackers

paper towels

SALADS

AMBROSIA SALAD

3/4 cup diced pared orange

1/2 cup green grapes, halved

3 Tablespoons lemon juice

1/2 cup mayonnaise

2 bananas, peeled and sliced

1/4 cup pitted dates, cut

1/2 cup heavy cream, whipped

1/4 cup flaked coconut

lettuce leaves or other greens

1. Combine fruit in large bowl.
2. Sprinkle with lemon juice.
3. Fold whipped cream into mayonnaise in a small bowl.
4. Fold cream mixture into fruit mixture.
5. Serve on greens.
6. Top with coconut.

EQUIPMENT NEEDED

2 bowls

cutting board

measuring spoons

electric mixer

knife

measuring cups

serving spoon

paper towels

AVOCADO AND CITRUS SALAD

3 avocados, diced   3 cups grapefruit chunks
lettuce   Spicy Fruit Dressing

1. Arrange avocado and grapefruit on lettuce.
2. Serve with dressing that has been blended together as follows:

Spicy Fruit Dressing

1/2 cup grapefruit juice   1/4 cup honey
2 Tablespoons wine vinegar   1/2 teaspoon onion salt
1/2 teaspoon cardamom

1. Place ingredients in a small bowl and blend together with a whisk or a fork.

EQUIPMENT NEEDED

2 bowls   measuring cups
measuring spoons   2 spoons
spatula   knife
cutting board   whisk or fork
serving dish   paper towels

COOL APPLE SALAD

2 Granny Smith apples

1 cucumber

1/2 cup halved seedless grapes

1/2 cup plain yogurt

1 Tablespoon lemon juice

1 Tablespoon fresh mint

1/4 cup sunflower seeds

lettuce or other greens

1. Cut, core, and slice apples into narrow strips and place in bowl. Mix with yogurt to prevent apple from turning brown.
2. Peel cucumber and cut into narrow strips.
3. Mix with remaining ingredients except seeds.
4. Toss lightly and sprinkle with seeds on serving.

EQUIPMENT NEEDED

cutting board

bowl

measuring cups

paper towels

knife

measuring spoons

spoon

FRESH FRUIT BOWL WITH CARDAMOM DRESSING

2 cantaloupes   15 to 20 seedless grapes

1 grapefruit   1 kiwi

2 bananas   1 pint strawberries

1. Prepare cardamom dressing and set aside.
2. Peel melon and cut into bite size pieces. Place in a large bowl.
3. Peel and section grapefruit. Add to melon.
4. Slice bananas and grapes. Add to above fruit.
5. Peel, quarter, and slice kiwi. Add to above fruit.
6. In large bowl, toss fruit with dressing and serve.

CARDAMOM DRESSING

1 8 oz. cream cheese   3 Tablespoons lemon juice

1/4 cup milk   3/4 teaspoon cardamom

3 Tablespoons sugar

1. In small bowl, mix by hand with a whisk or by mixer at low speed.
2. Increase speed to medium and beat until smooth.

EQUIPMENT NEEDED

2 bowls   mixer

1/4 cup measure   measuring spoons

spatula   large spoon

knife   cutting board

whisk   paper towels

FRUIT SALAD WITH YOGURT DRESSING

2 cantaloupes	15 to 20 grapes
1 grapefruit	1 kiwi
2 bananas	1 pint strawberries
other seasonal fresh fruits	lettuce or other greens

1. Peel, seed and cut cantaloupes and place in large bowl.
2. Peel grapefruit and remove flesh from sections and add to large bowl.
3. Peel and slice banana. Add to other fruit and mix to prevent browning.
4. Add remaining fruit and cut if necessary.

YOGURT DRESSING

1 cup plain yogurt	2 Tablespoons mayonnaise
dash of lemon juice	dash of salt

1. Mix ingredients together in small bowl and add to fruit.

EQUIPMENT NEEDED

knife	cutting board
bowl	small bowl
measuring spoons	measuring cup
serving spoon	paper towels

SOUR CREAM POTATO SALAD

1/4 cup sour cream

1/4 cup mayonnaise

3 cups cooked potatoes,
   peeled and diced

salt and pepper to taste

1/2 teaspoon celery seed

1 teaspoon chopped onion

lettuce

1. Prepare potatoes and place in a large bowl.
2. Mix sour cream and mayonnaise, add to potatoes.
3. Mix in other ingredients. (If time, cool thoroughly.)
4. Heap onto bed of lettuce.
5. Serve.

EQUIPMENT NEEDED

cutting board

bowl

measuring spoons

spatula

paper towels

knife

measuring cups

wooden spoon

serving bowl

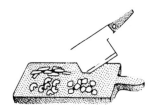

WALDORF SALAD

2 cups diced apples

1 cup diced celery

1/2 cup broken walnuts or raisins

1/4 cup mayonnaise

1 Tablespoon sugar

1/2 tsp. lemon juice

dash of salt

1. Combine apples, celery, and nuts or raisins.
2. Blend mayonnaise, sugar, lemon juice, and salt.
3. Fold into apple mixture.
4. Serve with or without lettuce.

CHEESE STICKS II

1 stick of 1/2 pkg. pie crust mix

1/2 cup shredded Cheddar cheese

1/8 teaspoon dry mustard

1 teaspoon paprika

1. Place ingredients in freezer zip lock bag plus the amount of water stated on the package.
2. Pass among the people and have them squeeze the bag to mix.
3. Place contents on lightly floured waxed paper and roll thin.
4. Cut 1/2 " wide and 4" long strips.
5. Bake on ungreased sheet at 425°F for 10 to 12 minutes.

EQUIPMENT NEEDED

measuring cups

spoon

bowl

rolling pin

oven

measuring spoons

knife

cutting board

waxed paper

serving dish

WATERMELON BOAT

1 watermelon   1 cantaloupe

2 peaches   1 bunch white grapes

1 kiwi fruit   3 Tablespoons lemon juice

1. Wash all fruit.
2. Using sharp knife, cut watermelon sawtooth fashion on top 1/3 of watermelon or cut into interesting shape. To relieve the inside pressure, make a x cut in the part of the watermelon you are going to remove before cutting into melon or it may split.
3. Place watermelon flesh into large bowl. Remove seeds and cut into balls or cubes.
4. Peel and cut cantaloupe, seed and cut into cubes or balls.
5. Peel, pit, and slice peaches.
6. Prepare remaining fruit and mix all fruit together.
7. Sprinkle with lemon juice.
8. Arrange in melon boat and serve.

EQUIPMENT NEEDED

knife   bowl

melon ball maker   cutting board

spoon   paper towels

BREADS

APPLE FRITTERS

1 cup flour

1 teaspoon baking powder

1/2 teaspoon salt

1 Tablespoon melted margarine

2 Tablespoons sugar

1 egg, slightly beaten

1/2 cup milk

3 large apples

1. Mix dry ingredients in small bowl.
2. Combine egg, milk and margarine in large bowl and stir into dry ingredients.
3. Pare, core, and cut apples into crosswise slices.
4. Dip each piece into batter and fry for 3 to 4 minutes or until golden brown in electric frying pan.
5. Serve with powdered sugar.

EQUIPMENT NEEDED

electric frying pan

measuring cups

spoon

cutting board

pancake turner

paper towels

2 bowls

measuring spoons

spatula

knife

serving plates

APPLE PUFFED PANCAKE

6 eggs(8 egg whites and 2 eggs)   1/2 teaspoon salt

1 1/2 cups milk   1/4 teaspoon cinnamon

1 cup flour   1/2 cup margarine

3 Tablespoons sugar   2 apples

1 teaspoon vanilla   2 Tablespoons brown sugar

1. Preheat oven to 425°F.
2. In blender or with beater, mix eggs, milk, flour, sugar, vanilla, salt and cinnamon until blended.
3. Melt margarine in 13"x9" baking dish.*
4. Add apple slices.
5. Return to oven until sizzling.
6. Remove dish from oven, pour batter over apples and sprinkle with brown sugar.
7. Bake 20 minutes or until puffed and brown.
8. Serve immediately.

*An electric frying pan can be used in place of an oven, but it will not brown as well.

EQUIPMENT NEEDED

blender   baking pan

knife   measuring cups

measuring spoons   spatula

spoon   pancake turner

oven or electric frying pan   paper towels

CHEDDAR-CHUTNEY SHORTBREAD

1 cup flour	1 teaspoon ginger
1/4 pound sharp cheddar cheese	1/2 teaspoon salt
1/4 cup margarine	1 egg
3 Tablespoons chutney	1/2 cup milk

1. Shred cheese.
2. Combine flour, cheese, margarine, ginger, and salt and cut into fine crumbs.
3. Add egg and milk until dough holds together.
4. On floured waxed paper, pat into ball and then in 1 1/4" thick log.
5. Slice log into 18 equally thick rounds.
6. Lay 1/2" apart on ungreased baking sheet.
7. In center of each round, make a depression and fill with 1/2 teaspoon of chutney.
8. Bake at 425°F for 12 to 15 minutes or until browned on edges.

EQUIPMENT NEEDED

grater	waxed paper
bowl	measuring cups
measuring spoons	pastry blender
spoon	spatula
knife	baking sheet
oven	teaspoon
serving plate	paper towels

CHEESE SCONES

2 cups flour

3 teaspoons baking powder

1 teaspoon baking soda

1/2 teaspoon thyme

1/4 teaspoon salt

6 Tablespoons margarine

2 cups shredded cheddar cheese

2 eggs

1/2 cup buttermilk

1. Preheat oven to 400°F.
2. In large bowl, mix dry ingredients.
3. Cut margarine into dry ingredients until coarse crumbs. Stir in shredded cheese.
4. In small bowl, blend with fork the eggs and buttermilk.
5. Stir into flour mixture to blend.
6. Knead on floured waxed paper 15 times.
7. Flatten into a circle and cut into wedges.
8. Place on ungreased sheet 2" apart.
9. Bake 18 to 20 minutes or until slightly browned.

EQUIPMENT NEEDED

2 bowls

measuring spoons

spoon

pancake turner

waxed paper

oven

paper towels

measuring cups

fork

spatula

pastry blender

baking sheets

serving plate

CORN PANCAKES

1 medium size red bell pepper

2 Tablespoons margarine

1 1/2 cups fresh corn kernels

1/2 cup minced onion

2/3 cup yellow cornmeal

1/3 cup chicken broth

4 eggs

3 Tablespoons parmesan cheese

1/2 teaspoon salt

1. Cut, seed and dice red pepper.
2. In an electric frying pan, cook pepper in margarine until limp and slightly browned. Set pepper aside.
3. Add corn and onion to pan and cook until limp and slightly browned.
4. In bowl, mix remaining ingredients and add corn mixture, then peppers.
5. Heat fry pan to 400°F. Lightly grease with salad oil. Spoon 2 Tablespoons of batter on pan allowing 1 inch between cakes.
6. Flatten cakes slightly. Cook until golden brown and turn once.
7. Serve hot. Add dab of margarine on top of each cake.

EQUIPMENT NEEDED

knife

electric frying pan

measuring cups

bowl

spatula

paper towels

cutting board

pancake turner

measuring spoons

electric mixer or spoon

serving plate

CORNMEAL CRACKERS

1 3/4 cups flour

1/2 cup cornmeal

2 teaspoons baking powder

1 teaspoon salt

1 Tablespoon sugar

1 egg, lightly beaten

3/4 cup sour cream

1 5 ounce jar cheese spread

2 Tablespoons caraway seeds

2 Tablespoons melted margarine

2 Tablespoons poppy seeds

1. Preheat oven to 400°F.
2. Mix together flour, cornmeal, baking powder, salt, and sugar.
3. Gradually add egg and sour cream until well mixed.
4. Turn onto lightly floured waxed paper and knead gently. Roll to 1/8" thick.
5. Spread half with cheese spread and sprinkle with caraway seeds. Cut into squares..
6. Spread remaining half with melted margarine and sprinkle with poppy seeds. Cut into squares.
7. Place on ungreased baking sheet and bake 8 to 10 minutes.

EQUIPMENT NEEDED

bowl

measuring spoons

spatula

rolling pin

knife

baking sheets

paper towels

measuring cups

spoon

pancake turner

waxed paper

oven

serving plate

COTTAGE CHEESE PANCAKES

4 eggs, separated

1/4 cup flour

1/4 cup small curd cottage cheese

1/4 cup sour cream

dash of salt

1. In medium bowl, beat egg yolks, flour, cottage cheese,and sour cream until blended.
2. In small bowl, beat egg whites with salt until stiff. (Be sure the beater is very clean)
3. Gently fold egg whites in egg yolk mixture.
4. Spoon onto moderately hot, greased griddle or electric frying pan.
5. When underside is brown, turn pancake over and cook until golden.
6. Serve with :

HONEY BUTTER

1/4 cup honey

2 Tablespoons cream or milk

2 Tablespoons margarine

Beat or whisk together the above ingredients.

EQUIPMENT NEEDED

electric frying pan

3 spoons

measuring cups

spatula

paper towels

3 bowls

mixer

measuring spoons

pancake turner

serving dish

DATE AND ORANGE SCONES

2 cups flour

3 teaspoons baking powder

1/2 teaspoon salt

1/2 cup chopped dates

1 teaspoon orange peel

1 Tablespoon sugar

1/2 cup shortening

2 eggs, beaten

1/2 cup milk

1. Mix dry ingredients.
2. Cut in 5 Tablespoons shortening.
3. Beat together eggs, milk, and stir into dry ingredients.
4. Fold in dates and orange peel.
5. Place on floured waxed paper and divide into 2 equal parts.
6. Pat each in 6 1/2" rounds and cut into wedges 1/2" thick.
7. Place scones on sprayed baking sheets and brush tops with remaining melted shortening.
8. Bake at 425°F for 15 minutes. Serve warm.

EQUIPMENT NEEDED

2 bowls

measuring spoons

spatula

oven

pastry blender

serving tray

non-stick spray

measuring cups

wooden spoon

knife

waxed paper

paper towels

baking tray

DATE AND POPPY SEED PANCAKES

1 cup buttermilk

1/2 cup finely chopped dates

2 Tablespoons melted butter

1 egg

3/4 cup flour

2 Tablespoons poppy seeds

1 teaspoon baking soda

1/2 teaspoon salt

oil

powdered sugar

1. Stir buttermilk, dates, butter, and eggs together in a small bowl and blend well.
2. Combine flour, poppy seeds, soda, and salt in a large bowl and stir into liquid.
3. Mix lightly with fork.
4. Heat electric frying pan medium high.
5. Brush with oil.
6. Spoon onto frying pan but leave room between pancakes so they do not touch each other while baking.
7. Bake on both sides.
8. Dust with powdered sugar and serve with fruit (optional).

EQUIPMENT NEEDED

electric frying pan

2 bowls

spoon

measuring spoons

paper towels

2 spatulas

fork

measuring cups

serving plate

DATE-ORANGE SCONES

1 package piecrust mix   1 Tablespoon sugar

1 1/2 teaspoons baking powder   1 teaspoon orange peel

1/4 teaspoon baking soda   1/2 cup chopped dates

1/2 cup sour milk*

1. In medium bowl, mix dry ingredients.
2. Make well in dry ingredients, add milk and dates, then mix with a fork.
3. Let stand 5 minutes.
4. On well floured waxed paper, knead dough gently 10 to 12 strokes.
5. Pat dough to a circle of 1/2" thickness.
6. Cut into 8 to 10 wedges.
7. Bake on greased baking sheet at 450°F for 12 to 15 minutes.

* To sour fresh milk, add 1 1/2 tsp. lemon juice and let stand for 5 minutes.

EQUIPMENT NEEDED

bowl   1/2 cup measure

measuring spoons   waxed paper

flour   non-stick spray

baking sheet   knife

serving dish   paper towels

oven   fork

spatula

GINGERBREAD WAFFLES

1 cup flour

3/4 cup whole wheat flour

1 Tablespoon baking powder

1/2 teaspoon ginger

1/4 teaspoon salt

1/4 teaspoon ground cloves

2 slightly beaten eggs

1 1/3 cups milk

1/2 cup oil

1/3 cup molasses

1. Lightly grease waffle iron and preheat.
2. In a large bowl, combine flours, baking powder, spices, and salt.
3. In small bowl, beat together eggs, milk, oil, and molasses.
4. Add liquid ingredients to dry ingredients and stir until all ingredients are moist.
5. Pour enough batter into iron to almost cover the baking surface, spread slightly, and bake 4 to 5 minutes until iron stops steaming.
6. Serve immediately with fruit spread or maple syrup.

EQUIPMENT NEEDED

2 bowls

measuring spoons

spatula

waffle iron

maple syrup

non-stick spray

measuring cups

wooden spoon

whisk

serving dish

paper towels

fork

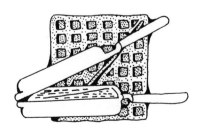

HONEY-APPLE PANCAKES

1 1/4 cups flour

2 teaspoons baking powder

1/4 cup apple pie spices

1/8 teaspoon baking soda

1/4 teaspoon salt

1 egg

3/4 cup apple juice

2 Tablespoons honey

1 Tablespoon oil

1. In a large bowl, stir flour, baking powder, baking soda, salt, and apple pie spice.
2. In a small bowl, mix egg, apple juice, honey and oil.
3. Add to flour mixture, stir until blended.
4. For each pancake, pour a small amount of batter on lightly greased frying pan.
   Bake 2 to 3 minutes, turn and bake for 2 more minutes and serve.

EQUIPMENT NEEDED

electric frying pan

pancake turner

measuring spoons

spatula

serving dish

2 bowls

measuring cups

spoon

non-stick spray

paper towels

HOT CROSS BUNS

Refrigerated biscuits   sugar

cinnamon   raisins

tubes of icing

(Quantities will vary according to the number of people participating and the number of buns to be consumed by each person.)

1. Mix each biscuit with cinnamon, sugar, and raisins. This can be done in individual freezer weight ziplock bags. Each person can be given one to mix without opening the bag.
2. Grease the pan. Place buns on pan and bake 10 to 15 minutes at 450°F.
3. Ice in form of cross. Serve warm.

EQUIPMENT NEEDED

ziplock bags   3 bowls

2 spoons   knife

oven   non-stick spray

paper towels   baking sheets

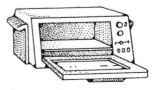

ORANGE BLOSSOM FRENCH TOAST

12 slices bread (day old)   2 Tablespoons orange peel

3 eggs   1/2 teaspoon salt

1/2 cup milk   1/4 cup margarine

1/3 cup orange juice

1. Slightly beat eggs and mix in milk, orange juice, peel and salt.
2. Dip bread into batter.
3. Heat margarine in electric frying pan.
4. Cook on both sides until golden.
5. Serve with orange syrup.

ORANGE SYRUP

1/2 cup brown sugar   1 1/2 teaspoons orange rind

1/4 cup orange juice

1. Mix ingredients and simmer 5 minutes.
2. Serve warm.

EQUIPMENT NEEDED

hot plate   electric frying pan

measuring cups   measuring spoons

bowl   2 spoons

plate   knife

fork   pancake turner

pan   waxed paper

paper towels

PEACH GRIDDLECAKES

2 cups flour

3 teaspoons baking powder

1/2 teaspoon salt

2 Tablespoons melted margarine

1 Tablespoon sugar

1 egg, well beaten

1 1/2 cups milk

1 cup chopped peaches

cinnamon and sugar mixture

1. Mix dry ingredients in a large bowl.
2. Combine egg and milk in a large bowl; add dry ingredients and beat until smooth.
3. Add melted margarine.
4. Add peaches and mix well.
5. Bake on ungreased, hot griddle.
6. Serve hot with butter and cinnamon sugar.

EQUIPMENT NEEDED

2 bowls

measuring spoons

wooden spoon

knife

paper towels

1 cup measure

2 spatulas, rubber and metal

electric frying pan

cutting board

serving plate

POTATO PANCAKES

2 cups grated potatoes   2 teaspoons grated onion

3 eggs   1 teaspoon salt

1/2 Tablespoon flour   oil

1. Peel and grate potatoes into a large bowl.
2. Remove excess moisture.
3. In a small bowl, beat eggs and stir them into potatoes.
4. Combine flour and salt and add to potatoes.
5. Add onions.
6. Heat oil and place spoonful of mixture on the electric frying pan.
7. Brown on both sides and serve with applesauce.

APPLESAUCE

1 pound apples   sugar or sweetener

cinnamon

1. Quarter and core apples. Peel apples if you are going to force through sieve.
2. Cook with small amount of water.
3. Blend or force through sieve.
4. Add sugar and cinnamon to taste.

EQUIPMENT NEEDED

2 bowls   grater

measuring spoons   2 spoons

spatula   electric frying pan

pancake turner   waxed paper

2 cup measure   serving dish

paper towels   pan

hot plate   blender or sieve

small bowl

PUFFED PANCAKE WITH STRAWBERRIES

6 eggs

1 cup milk

1/4 cup orange juice or Triple Sec

1 cup flour

1/2 teaspoon salt

1/4 pound margarine

1/2 cup sugar

powdered sugar

1. Mix eggs, milk, juice, sugar, flour and salt in a large bowl with mixer. Batter will be lumpy.
2. Preheat oven to 425°F. (If using an electric frying pan, heat to 375ºF.)
3. Melt margarine in 13"x9" pan or in an electric frying pan and add batter.
4. Bake 20 minutes or until puffy and brown.
5. Remove pancake from oven, sprinkle with powdered sugar, and serve with sauce immediately.

STRAWBERRY SAUCE

2 (10 ounce) packages frozen strawberries

3 Tablespoons orange juice or Triple Sec

1. Make sauce by heating strawberries until hot and add orange juice.

EQUIPMENT NEEDED

bowl

measuring cups

spatula

13"x9" pan or electric frying pan

pan

paper towels

mixer

measuring spoons

oven

hot plate

spoon

SCOTCH CREAM SCONES

2 cups flour	1 Tablespoon sugar
3 teaspoons baking powder	1/2 cup margarine
1/2 teaspoon salt	2 eggs, beaten
1/2 cup golden raisins	1/2 cup light cream

1. Preheat oven to 425ºF and spray baking sheets with non-stick spray.
2. Mix dry ingredients in large bowl.
3. Cut in 5 Tablespoons margarine.
4. Beat together eggs and cream and stir into dry ingredients.
5. Fold in raisins.
6. Place on floured surface and divide into 2 equal parts.
7. Pat each part into 6 1/2" round. and cut into wedges or pat 1/2" thick and cut into diamond shapes.
8. Place on greased pan and brush tops with remaining melted margarine.
9. Bake for 15 minutes or until browned.

EQUIPMENT NEEDED

2 bowls	measuring cups
measuring spoons	spoon
spatula	knife
pastry blender	waxed paper
baking sheets	oven
non-stick spray	serving plate
paper towels	

SPICED PUMPKIN PANCAKES

2 cups flour

3 Tablespoons sugar

2 teaspoons baking powder

1 teaspoon baking soda

1 teaspoon cinnamon

1/2 teaspoon nutmeg

1/2 teaspoon salt

1 3/4 cups milk

1 cup pumpkin

2 eggs

2 Tablespoons oil

margarine

syrup

1. Mix flour and other dry ingredients in a large bowl.
2. In another bowl, beat milk, pumpkin, eggs and oil to blend.
3. Add flour mixture and stir until moistened.
4. On a preheated electric frying pan, pour small amount of batter at least 1 " apart.
5. Turn, after bubbles form, and brown.
6. Serve with margarine and syrup.

EQUIPMENT NEEDED

2 bowls

spatula

measuring cup

serving plate

pancake turner

electric frying pan

spoon

measuring spoons

knife

paper towels

WHEAT AND HERB SCONES

1 1/2 cups flour

1 1/2 cups whole wheat flour

1 Tablespoon baking powder

1 teaspoon dry basil leaves

dash of salt

1/2 teaspoon dried oregano

1/2 teaspoon dried thyme

1/2 cup margarine

2 eggs

3/4 cup milk

1. Preheat oven to 400°F and spray baking sheets with non-stick spray.
2. Mix dry ingredients in a large bowl and cut in butter until coarse crumbs.
3. Beat eggs and milk together and **set aside 2 Tablespoonfuls**.
4. Add to flour mixture and stir until evenly moistened.
5. Scrape onto floured waxed paper and knead about 6 times.
6. Divide dough into 2 equal parts. Pat half into 3/4" thick round 5 to 6" in diameter.
7. Place on greased baking sheet.
8. With knife, cut each round not quite through to form 6 wedges.
9. Brush with reserved egg mixture. Bake for 18 minutes or until browned.

EQUIPMENT NEEDED

2 bowls

measuring spoons

spatula

waxed paper

baking sheets

non-stick spray

paper towels

measuring cups

spoon

pastry blender

knife

oven

serving plate

YOGURT SCONES

1 1/4 cups flour

1/2 cup whole wheat flour

1 Tablespoon sugar

2 teaspoons baking powder

1/2 teaspoon baking soda

1/4 cup margarine

1/2 cup lemon-flavor yogurt

1/3 cup mashed banana

1/2 cup blueberries

1 egg

1. Preheat oven to 425ºF and spray baking sheets with non-stick spray.
2. Mix dry ingredients in large bowl and cut in margarine.
3. Add eggs, yogurt, banana, and blueberries.
4. Place on floured surface and divide into 2 equal parts.
5. Pat each part into 6 1/2" round and cut into wedges or pat 1/2" thick and cut into diamond shapes.
6. Place on baking sheets and bake for 15 minutes or until browned.
7. Split each portion and spread with margarine.

EQUIPMENT NEEDED

2 bowls

measuring spoons

spatula

fork

waxed paper

oven

serving plate

measuring cups

spoon

knife

pastry blender

baking sheets

non-stick spray

paper towels

MUFFINS

APPLE MUFFINS

2 cups flour

1/2 cup sugar

2 1/4 teaspoons baking powder

1/2 teaspoon salt

1 teaspoon cinnamon

1 egg

2/3 cup milk

3 Tablespoons oil

1 teaspoon lemon peel

1 teaspoon vanilla

1 cup grated apple

1. Preheat oven to 400ºF and spray muffin pans with non-stick spray.
2. In a large bowl, mix dry ingredients.
3. In a small bowl, beat egg, add milk, oil, lemon peel, and vanilla.
4. Stir in dry ingredients and mix until moistened.
5. Fold in grated apple.
6. Spoon into muffin cups.
7. Bake for 15 to 20 minutes or until golden brown.

EQUIPMENT NEEDED

2 bowls

measuring cups

spoon

muffin tins

non-stick spray

paper towels

waxed paper

grater

measuring spoons

spatula

oven

serving plate

knife

APPLE-ALLSPICE MUFFINS

1/4 cup +2 Tablespoons margarine

3/4 cup brown sugar substitute

1 egg

1 3/4 cups flour

2 teaspoons baking powder

1 teaspoon allspice

1/4 teaspoon salt

3/4 cup milk

1 cup peeled chopped apple

1. Cream 1/4 cup margarine and gradually add 1/2 cup brown sugar beating until light and fluffy in a large bowl.
2. Add egg and mix well.
3. Combine 1 1/2 cup flours, 1/2 teaspoon allspice, baking powder, and salt. Add to creamed mixture alternately with milk until moist.
4. Stir in chopped apple.
5. Spoon into greased muffin tins 2/3 full.
6. Combine 1/4 cup brown sugar, 1/4 cup flour, 1/2 teaspoon allspice then cut in 2 Tablespoons margarine with pastry blender to resemble coarse meal.
7. Sprinkle over top of muffins.
8. Bake at 400°F 20 minutes or until lightly browned.

EQUIPMENT NEEDED

oven

measuring cups

spoon

cutting board

muffin tins

pastry blender

paper towels

2 bowls

measuring spoons

spatula

knife

non-stick spray

serving plate

APPLE-CRANBERRY MUFFINS

1 3/4 cups + 2 Tablespoons flour

1/2 cup sugar

1 1/2 teaspoons baking powder

1/2 teaspoon baking soda

1/2 teaspoon salt

1 egg

3/4 cup milk

3/4 cup applesauce

1/4 cup margarine, melted

1 cup chopped cranberries

1/2 teaspoon cinnamon

1. Combine 1 3/4 cups flour, 1/4 cup sugar, baking powder, baking soda and salt.
2. In small bowl, combine egg, milk, applesauce and margarine.
3. Add to dry ingredients and mix until blended.
4. Mix chopped cranberries with 2 Tablespoons flour and fold into batter.
5. Spoon into greased muffin tins.
6. Combine 1/4 cup sugar and cinnamon and sprinkle over muffins.
7. Bake at 400°F 20 to 25 minutes or until browned.

EQUIPMENT NEEDED

2 bowls

measuring spoons

spatula

cutting board

oven

serving plate

measuring cups

spoon

muffin tins

knife

non-stick spray

paper towels

APPLE WALNUT MUFFINS

2 cups flour

2/3 cup sugar

2 1/4 teaspoons baking powder

3/4 teaspoon salt

1/4 teaspoon cinnamon

1 egg

2/3 cup milk

3 Tablespoons oil

1 teaspoon orange peel

3/4 teaspoon vanilla

1 cup chopped walnut(optional)

3/4 cup coarsely grated apple

1. Preheat oven at 400°F and spray muffin pans with non-stick spray.

2. Mix flour, sugar, salt, baking powder, salt, and cinnamon in a small bowl.

3. In a large bowl, beat egg with milk, oil, orange peel, and vanilla.

4. Stir into dry ingredients and mix until moistened.

5. Fold in walnuts and apple. Spoon into greased muffin cups.

6. Bake for 15 to 20 minutes or until golden brown.

EQUIPMENT NEEDED

2 bowls

measuring cups

spatula

cutting board

non-stick spray

paper towels

measuring spoons

2 spoons

knife

muffin tins

serving dish

APRICOT MUFFINS

1 1/2 cups flour

1/2 teaspoon salt

1 teaspoon baking soda

1 1/2 cups whole wheat flour

1/4 cup shortening

1/2 cup sugar

3/4 cup apricot pulp

1/4 cup apricot juice

1 cup buttermilk

1 egg

1. Mix together flour, salt, and baking soda in a small bowl.
2. Add whole wheat flour.
3. Cream shortening with sugar in a large bowl.
4. Beat in egg.
5. Add apricot pulp and juice.
6. Add dry ingredients alternately with buttermilk.
7. Stir until blended.
8. Place in greased muffin tins.
9. Bake at 350°F for 20 minutes.

EQUIPMENT NEEDED

2 bowls

measuring cups

measuring spoons

wooden spoon

2 spatulas

serving plate

muffin tins

non-stick spray

oven

paper towels

knife

AVOCADO MUFFINS

1 egg   1/2 teaspoon baking soda
1/2 cup mashed avocado   1/2 teaspoon baking powder
1/2 cup buttermilk   1/4 teaspoon salt
1/3 cup oil   (3/4 cup chopped pecans)
2 cups flour   butter
3/4 cup sugar

1. Preheat oven to 350°F and spray muffin tins.
2. Mix egg, avocado, buttermilk, and oil until blended in a large bowl.
3. Add flour, sugar, baking soda, baking powder and salt and mix until blended.
   Add chopped pecans if desired.
4. Fill muffin tins 2/3 full.
5. Bake 25 minutes or until browned.
6. Serve with butter.

EQUIPMENT NEEDED

2 bowls   measuring cups
measuring spoons   spoon
fork   spatula
cutting board   knife
oven   non-stick spray
muffin tins   serving plate
paper towels

BANANA POPPY SEED MUFFINS

2 ripe bananas, peeled

1 egg

3/4 cup sugar

1/4 cup oil

2 teaspoons grated orange peel

2 cups flour

1 1/2 Tablespoons poppy seeds

2 teaspoons baking powder

1/2 teaspoon salt

1. Puree bananas or mash with a fork.
2. In medium bowl, mix bananas, egg, sugar, oil and orange peel until well blended.
3. In large bowl, combine flour, poppy seeds, baking powder, and salt.
4. Stir banana mixture into flour mixture until moist.
5. Spoon batter into greased mini muffin tins.
6. Bake at 375ºF for 15 to 20 minutes.

EQUIPMENT NEEDED

2 bowls

measuring cups

spatula

muffin tins

oven

paper towels

measuring spoons

wooden spoon

fork

non-stick spray

serving dish

BLACK AND ORANGE MUFFINS

2 cups flour

1/2 cup sugar

1 Tablespoon baking powder

1 teaspoon salt

1 teaspoon grated orange peel

3/4 cup orange juice

1/3 cup oil

1 egg, beaten

1/2 cup cocoa

1. Preheat oven to 400°F and spray muffin tins with non-stick spray.
2. In a large bowl, combine flour, sugar, baking powder and salt.
3. In a small bowl, combine orange juice, oil, and egg.
4. Stir liquid ingredients, into dry ingredients until moistened.
5. Place half the batter into a small bowl and stir in cocoa.
6. Stir orange peel into remaining batter.
7. Spoon orange batter into half of each cup and fill the other side with cocoa mixture.
8. Bake 20 minutes or until browned.

EQUIPMENT NEEDED

2 bowls

measuring spoons

spatula

waxed paper

non-stick spray

serving plate

measuring cups

2 spoons

grater

muffin tins

oven

paper towels

BLUEBERRY MUFFINS

1 3/4 cups flour

1/4 cup sugar

2 1/2 teaspoons baking powder

3/4 teaspoon salt

1 egg

3/4 cup milk

1/3 cup oil

1 cup blueberries

1. Mix flour, sugar, baking powder, and salt in a large bowl.
2. Make well in center.
3. Combine egg, milk, and oil in a small bowl.
4. Add all at once to dry ingredients.
5. Stir quickly until all ingredients are moist.
6. Stir in blueberries.
7. Fill greased muffin tins 2/3 full.
8. Bake at 400°F about 20 to 25 minutes.

EQUIPMENT NEEDED

2 bowls

measuring spoons

spatula

oven

serving plate

measuring cups

spoon

muffin tins

non-stick spray

paper towels

BLUEBERRY ORANGE MUFFINS

2 1/4 cups flour

2/3 cup sugar

2 teaspoons baking powder

1 teaspoon baking soda

1/2 teaspoon salt

1/2 cup margarine

3/4 cup plain yogurt

1 small orange, peeled, seeded and
   chopped with juice

2 teaspoons grated orange peel

2 eggs, beaten

1 1/2 cups fresh blueberries

1. In large bowl, whisk together flour, sugar, baking powder, baking soda, and salt.
2. Cut in margarine until the texture is like fine crumbs.
3. In small bowl, combine yogurt, orange, and orange peel until blended and stir in eggs.
4. Make well in center of flour mixture. Pour in egg mixture and stir until moist. Fold in blueberries.
5. Spoon batter in greased muffin tins and bake at 400°F for 15 to 20 minutes or until lightly browned. Cool and serve.

EQUIPMENT NEEDED

2 bowls

measuring spoons

spatula

muffin tins

oven

paper towels

measuring cups

spoon

pastry blender

non-stick spray

serving dish

BRAN MUFFINS

1 1/4 cups flour

3 teaspoons baking powder

1/4 teaspoon salt

2 Tablespoons sugar

1 cup raisins

1 cup bran

1 cup milk

1 egg

3 Tablespoons oil

1. Mix flour, baking powder, salt, and sugar in a small bowl.
2. Measure bran and milk into large bowl. Stir and let stand 2 minutes.
3. Add egg and oil.
4. Add flour mixture and raisins and stir until blended.
5. Fill muffin tins 2/3 full.
6. Bake at 400°F for 20 minutes or until browned.

EQUIPMENT NEEDED

2 bowls

measuring spoons

spatula

muffin tins

non-stick spray

paper towels

measuring cups

spoon

knife

oven

serving plate

CORN MUFFINS

3/4 cup flour

2 1/2 teaspoons baking powder

2 Tablespoons sugar

3/4 teaspoon salt

1 egg

3 Tablespoons melted margarine

1 cup milk

1 1/4 cups cornmeal

1. Beat egg in a large bowl.
2. Add and beat in melted margarine and milk.
3. Combine flour, baking powder, sugar, salt and cornmeal in a small bowl.
4. Add to liquid and mix quickly.
5. Place in greased muffin tins filled 2/3 full.
6. Bake at 425°F for 20 to 25 minutes or until browned.

EQUIPMENT NEEDED

2 bowls

measuring spoons

spatula

muffin tins

serving plate

paper towels

measuring cups

spoon

knife

oven

knife

non-stick spray

CRANBERRY-APRICOT TEA CAKES

1/2 cups boiling water

3/8 cup dried apricots

1/4 cup margarine

3/8 cup sugar

1 egg

3/4 teaspoon vanilla

3/4 cup flour

1 teaspoon baking powder

1/4 teaspoon baking soda

1/4 teaspoon salt

1/2 cup chopped cranberries

powdered sugar for garnish

1. In medium bowl, soak apricots in boiling water for 15 minutes.   Drain, reserving 3/8 cup liquid. Chop apricots.
2. Preheat oven to 375°F. Spray with non-stick spray and flour tins.
3. In large bowl, cream margarine and sugar until light and fluffy.
4. Beat in egg; beat in vanilla.
5. Alternately add dry ingredients and the apricot liquid, beating well after each addition.
6. Fold in cranberries and apricots.
7. Spoon batter into muffin tins, filling 3/4 full.
8. Bake 20 to 23 minutes. Cool on rack for 5 minutes, then remove from pan. Dust with powdered sugar.

EQUIPMENT NEEDED

oven

muffin tins

two bowls

measuring cups

measuring spoons

spoon

spatula

knife

cutting board

non-stick spray

paper towels

serving dish

DATE AND BRAN MUFFINS

1/4 cup flour

1 Tablespoon baking powder

1/4 teaspoon salt

2 Tablespoons sugar

1/2 cup chopped dates

1 1/4 cups skim milk

1 egg

2 Tablespoons oil

1 1/2 cups bran

1. Stir together flour, baking powder, salt, sugar, and dates in small bowl.
2. Mix bran and milk in large bowl. Let stand 1 to 2 minutes or until bran is softened.
3. Add egg and oil to bran mixture. Beat well.
4. Add flour mixture and stir until all ingredients are moistened.
5. Filled greased muffin tins.
6. Bake at 400°F for 15 to 18 minutes.

EQUIPMENT NEEDED

bowl

measuring cups

spoon

knife

non-stick spray

oven

2 cup measure

measuring spoons

spatula

muffin tins

serving dish

paper towels

DOUBLE CORN MINI MUFFINS

1 cup flour	1/2 teaspoon salt
1 cup yellow cornmeal	1 8 1/2 ounce can creamed corn
2 Tablespoons brown sugar	1/2 cup buttermilk
1 Tablespoon baking powder	1 egg
1/2 teaspoon baking soda	1/2 cup margarine, melted

1. Preheat oven to 425°F. Spray muffin tins with non-stick spray.
2. Mix flour, cornmeal, brown sugar, baking powder, baking soda, and salt in large bowl.
3. Whisk creamed corn, buttermilk, and egg in small bowl.
4. Add melted margarine and whisk.
5. Form a well in dry ingredients and add wet ingredients and stir until moistened.
6. Spoon into muffin tins 3/4 full.
7. Bake until golden brown or 10 minutes.

EQUIPMENT NEEDED

2 bowls	measuring cups
measuring spoons	whisk
spoon	spatula
knife	muffin tins
oven	serving plate
paper towels	non-stick spray
can opener	

HONEY-LEMON MUFFINS

1 cup flour	1/2 cup whole wheat flour
1 teaspoon baking powder	1/4 teaspoon baking soda
1/4 teaspoon salt	1 egg
1/2 cup honey	1/4 cup lemon juice
1/2 teaspoon lemon peel	1/4 cup margarine, melted

1. Preheat oven to 375ºF and spray muffin tins with non-stick spray.
2. Stir together flours, baking powder, soda, and salt. Make a well.
3. Combine egg, honey, lemon peel, lemon juice, and margarine.
4. Add all at once to flour mixture and stir to moisten.
5. Fill muffin tins and bake at 375°F for 15 minutes.

EQUIPMENT NEEDED

oven	muffin tins
bowl	measuring cups
measuring spoons	spoon
spatula	non-stick spray
serving dish	paper towels

HOT CROSS MUFFINS

2 cups flour

3/4 cup sugar

2 teaspoons baking powder

1/2 teaspoon salt

1/4 teaspoon cinnamon

1 cup milk

1 egg, lightly beaten

1 teaspoon vanilla

1/2 teaspoon grated orange peel

1/4 teaspoon grated lemon peel

1 cup currants

1/8 teaspoon allspice

1/2 cup margarine, melted

GLAZE

1/3 cup confectioners' sugar

1 1/2 teaspoons freshly squeezed lemon juice or orange juice or water

1. Preheat oven to 375°F and spray muffin tins with non-stick spray.
2. In large bowl, mix flour, sugar, baking powder, salt, cinnamon, and allspice.
3. In small bowl, mix milk, margarine, egg, vanilla, orange and lemon peel.
4. Make a well in center of dry ingredients, add wet ingredients, and mix until all ingredients are moist. Stir in currants.
5. Spoon into greased muffin tins and bake 15 to 20 minutes.
6. Remove from tins and cool on rack.
7. Combine ingredients for glaze and drizzle over each muffin in form of a cross.

EQUIPMENT NEEDED

2 bowls

muffin tins

measuring spoons

spatula

paper towels

oven

measuring cups

spoon

serving dish

non-stick spray

JELLY MUFFINS

1 3/4 cups flour

1/4 cup sugar

2 1/2 teaspoons baking powder

1/2 teaspoon salt

1 well beaten egg

3/4 cup milk

1/3 cup oil or melted margarine

tart jelly

1. Mix flour, sugar, baking powder, and salt in a bowl and make a well.
2. Combine egg, milk and oil in small bowl.
3. Add liquid all at once to dry ingredients. Stir quickly until moistened.
4. Fill greased muffin tins 2/3 full. Top with a dot of tart jelly.
5. Bake at 400°F for 20 minutes or until browned.

EQUIPMENT NEEDED

2 bowls

measuring spoons

spoon

knife

non-stick spray

serving plate

measuring cups

fork

spatula

muffin tins

oven

paper towels

LEMON APPLE OAT MUFFINS

1 1/4 cups flour

1/2 cup brown sugar

1 1/2 teaspoons baking powder

1 teaspoon baking soda

1 teaspoon cinnamon

1/2 teaspoon salt

1 egg

1/2 cup evaporated milk

1/4 cup oil

2 Tablespoons lemon juice

3/4 cup oats

1 cup chopped apple

1/4 teaspoon nutmeg

LEMON GLAZE

1/2 cup confectioner's sugar

1 Tablespoon melted margarine

1 Tablespoon lemon juice

1. Combine flour, brown sugar, baking powder, baking soda, cinnamon, nutmeg and salt in a small bowl.
2. In a large bowl, beat egg, and stir in milk, oil, and lemon juice.
3. Add oats and mix well.
4. Add dry ingredients and apples. Stir until moistened.
5. Spoon into greased muffin tins.
6. Bake at 400°F for 20 minutes or until browned.
7. Prepare glaze and spoon over warm muffins.

EQUIPMENT NEEDED

2 bowls

measuring spoons

spatula

cutting board

non-stick spray

serving plate

measuring cups

2 spoons

knife

muffin tins

oven

paper towels

LEMON TEA MUFFINS

2 cups flour

2 teaspoons baking powder

1/2 teaspoon salt

1 cup margarine

3/4 cup sugar

1/2 cup lemon juice

1/4 cup chopped nuts (optional)

2 Tablespoons brown sugar

1/4 teaspoon nutmeg

4 eggs, separated

1. Preheat oven to 375°F and spray muffin tins with non-stick spray.
2. Measure and combine flour, baking powder, and salt in a small bowl.
3. Beat margarine and sugar until fluffy in a large bowl.
4. Add egg yolks and beat until light.
5. Add dry ingredients alternately with lemon juice.
6. Beat egg whites until stiff and fold into mixture in a small clean bowl.
7. Fill muffin tins 3/4 full.
8. Combine nuts, brown sugar and nutmeg and sprinkle on top.
9. Bake 15 to 20 minutes or until browned.

EQUIPMENT NEEDED

2 bowls

measuring spoons

spatula

non-stick spray

serving plate

paper towels

measuring cups

2 spoons

muffin tins

oven

knife

LEMON YOGURT-RAISIN TEA MUFFINS

1 1/2 cups flour

3/4 cup whole wheat flour

1/4 cup sugar

2 teaspoons baking powder

1/2 teaspoon baking soda

1/4 teaspoon salt

1 cup lemon yogurt

1/4 cup melted margarine

1 egg

3/4 cup raisins

1. Preheat oven to 350°F and spray muffin tins with non-stick spray.
2. Mix flours, sugar, baking powder, baking soda, and salt in large bowl.
3. Mix yogurt, margarine, and egg to blend well in small bowl.
4. Pour liquid into dry ingredients.
5. Add raisins and stir to moisten.
6. Fill muffin tins.
7. Bake 20 minutes or until lightly browned.

EQUIPMENT NEEDED

2 bowls

measuring spoons

spatula

cupcake tins

oven

paper towels

measuring cups

wooden spoon

knife

non-stick spray

serving dish

MEXICAN CORN MUFFINS

1 cup flour

1 cup cornmeal

3 teaspoons baking powder

1/2 teaspoon salt

1 egg

1/2 cup shredded cheese

1 cup skim milk

1/4 cup chopped onion

2 ounces pimento

1/3 cup melted margarine

2 Tablespoons chopped chilies

1/2 teaspoon garlic powder

1/2 cup canned corn

1. Combine flour, cornmeal, baking powder, salt, and garlic powder in a large bowl.
2. In a small bowl, combine egg, shredded cheese, milk, pimento, margarine, chilies, and corn.
3. Add liquid ingredients to dry ingredients and stir well until all ingredients are moist.
3. Pour into sprayed muffin tins.
4. Bake at 400°F for 20 minutes.
5. Serve warm.

EQUIPMENT NEEDED

bowl

measuring spoons

spatula

knife

muffin tins

serving plate

non-stick spray

measuring cups

spoon

cutting board

can opener

oven

paper towels

NECTARINE MUFFINS

1/2 cup melted margarine   1 1/2 cups flour
1/4 cup milk   1/2 cup sugar
1 egg   2 teaspoons baking powder
2 medium nectarines, diced (about 1 cup)   1 teaspoon cinnamon
1/4 teaspoon salt

1. Preheat oven to 400°F and spray muffin tins with non-stick spray.
2. Prepare Topping and set aside.
3. In large bowl, mix flour, sugar, baking powder, cinnamon and salt.
4. In small bowl, mix melted margarine, milk and egg.
5. Pour liquids into flour mixture and stir until moist.
6. Fold in nectarines.
7. Spoon into muffin tins, sprinkle topping on each muffin and bake 20 to 25 minutes.

TOPPING

1. In small bowl, combine 1/3 cup brown sugar, 1/4 cup flour, and 1 teaspoon cinnamon.
2. Add 2 Tablespoons melted margarine and stir until crumbs form.

EQUIPMENT NEEDED

3 bowls   measuring cups
measuring spoons   spoons
spatula   cutting board
knife   muffin tins
oven   non-stick spray
serving dish   paper towels

OATMEAL RAISIN MUFFINS

1 8 ounce can crushed pineapple

1 cup sour cream

1 egg

1/4 cup margarine, melted

1 1/2 cups flour

1 cup oats

1/2 cup sugar

1 Tablespoon baking powder

1 teaspoon cinnamon

1/2 teaspoon nutmeg

1/2 teaspoon salt

1 cup raisins

1. In small bowl, combine pineapple, sour cream, egg and margarine until blended.
2. In large bowl, combine remaining ingredients. Make a well.
3. Pour in pineapple mixture and stir until moistened.
4. Spoon into greased muffin tins.
5. Bake at 350°F about 20 minutes or until lightly browned.

EQUIPMENT NEEDED

2 bowls

measuring spoons

spatula

muffin tins

oven

paper towels

measuring cups

spoon

knife

non-stick spray

serving plate

PEPPERONI-CHEESE MINIS

1/4 lb. pepperoni	dash of pepper
1/2 cup flour	1 egg
1/2 cup cornmeal	1/2 cup milk
2 teaspoons baking powder	1/8 cup oil
dash of salt	1/4 cup shredded Monterey Jack cheese

2 Tablespoons diced green chilies

1. Preheat oven to 400°F. and spray mini-muffin tins with non-stick spray.
2. Cut 5 slices of pepperoni into 8 wedges. The remaining should be chopped.
3. Combine flour, cornmeal, baking powder, salt, and pepper in a large bowl.
4. In another bowl, combine egg, milk, and oil, then stir into dry ingredients until moist.
4. Fold in cheese, chilies, and chopped pepperoni.
5. Spoon into mini-muffin tins.
6. Top each muffin with a wedge of pepperoni, pressing halfway into muffin.
7. Bake 10 to 12 minutes or until golden brown.
8. Remove from pan immediately and serve warm.

EQUIPMENT NEEDED

cutting board	knife
2 bowls	measuring cups
measuring spoons	2 spoons
spatula	mini-muffin tins
non-stick spray	paper towels

PINEAPPLE CARROT RAISIN MUFFINS

2 cups flour

1/2 cup sugar

2 teaspoons baking powder

1/2 teaspoon cinnamon

1/4 teaspoon ginger

1/2 cup shredded carrots

1 8 ounce can crushed pineapple

2 eggs

1/2 cup melted margarine

1 teaspoon vanilla

1/2 cup raisins

1. Combine flour, sugar, baking powder, cinnamon and ginger in a large bowl.
2. Stir in carrots and raisins.
3. In small bowl, combine undrained pineapple, eggs, margarine, and vanilla.
4. Stir into dry ingredients until blended.
5. Spoon into greased muffin tins.
6. Bake at 375°F for 20 minutes.

EQUIPMENT NEEDED

2 bowls

measuring spoons

spatula

grater

muffin tins

non-stick spray

serving plate

measuring cups

spoon

knife

waxed paper

oven

can opener

paper towels

PUMPKIN MUFFINS

1 3/4 cups flour   1 teaspoon cinnamon

3/4 teaspoon salt   1 teaspoon nutmeg

1/2 cup sugar   1 cup pumpkin

2 teaspoons baking powder   1 cup raisins

2 eggs   2 Tablespoons orange rind

2 to 4 Tablespoons melted margarine   3/4 cup milk

1. Combine flour, salt, sugar, baking powder, cinnamon, and nutmeg in large bowl.
2. Beat eggs and add margarine, milk, and pumpkin in small bowl.
3. Add liquid ingredients to dry ingredients and mix until moistened.
4. Add raisins and orange rind.
5. Fill greased muffin tins 2/3 full.
6. Bake at 400°F 20 to 25 minutes.

EQUIPMENT NEEDED

2 bowls   measuring cups

measuring spoons   spoon

spatula   muffin tins

non-stick spray   oven

knife   serving plate

paper towels

SPA MUFFINS

1/2 cup raisins	1/4 teaspoon cloves
1 1/2 cups whole wheat flour	1 1/2 cups grated carrots
1 cup all bran	2/3 cup plain yogurt
1/3 cup sesame seeds	1/2 cup mashed banana
2 teaspoons cinnamon	1/2 cup orange juice
1 teaspoon baking soda	1/4 cup honey
1 teaspoon baking powder	2 Tablespoons oil
1/2 teaspoon allspice	1 Tablespoon grated lemon peel

1. Preheat oven to 350°F and spray muffin tins with non-stick spray.
2. Place raisins in bowl and cover with boiling water. Let stand 15 minutes. Drain and pat dry. (I do this ahead of time.)
3. Combine flour and the next 7 dry ingredients in large bowl. Make a well in center.
4. Blend raisins, carrots, and remaining ingredients in another bowl.
5. Pour raisin mixture in well, fold until everything is moistened.
6. Fill muffin tins and bake 20 minutes or until browned.
7. Cool slightly in tins then turn onto rack to cool.

EQUIPMENT NEEDED

3 bowls	measuring cups
measuring spoons	spoon
spatula	grater
waxed paper	fork
muffin tins	oven
non-stick spray	serving plate
racks	paper towels

STRAWBERRY MUFFINS

2 cups flour

3 teaspoons baking powder

1/2 teaspoon salt

1/4 cup sugar

1 egg, well beaten

1/2 cup milk

1 1/2 cups mashed strawberries

3 Tablespoons margarine, melted

1. Preheat oven to 425ºF and spray muffin tins with non-stick spray.
2. In large bowl, mix flour, baking powder, salt, and sugar and make well.
3. In small bowl, combine egg, milk, strawberries, and shortening.
4. Add liquid ingredients to flour mixture and stir until flour is moistened.
4. Fill muffin tins 2/3 full.
5. Bake for 20-25 minutes or until golden brown..

EQUIPMENT NEEDED

2 bowls

measuring spoons

spatula

oven

knife

2 cup measure

paper towels

measuring cups

spoon

non-stick spray

muffin tins

fork

serving dish

SURPRISE CHEESE MUFFINS

1 3/4 cups flour

1/4 cup sugar

1 Tablespoon baking powder

5 slices bacon, crisp, cooked, crumbled

3/4 cup milk

1 egg, beaten

1/3 cup oil or bacon drippings

small cubes of Swiss cheese

1. In medium bowl, combine flour, sugar, baking powder and bacon.

2. Add milk, egg, and oil, stirring just until moistened.

3. Spoon 1/2 of the batter into greased muffin tins.

4. Press a cheese cube into each cup and top with remaining batter, covering the cheese completely.

5. Bake at 400°F for 20 minutes or until browned.

6. Remove from pans and serve hot.

EQUIPMENT NEEDED

bowl

measuring spoons

spatula

cutting board

muffin tins

paper towels

measuring cups

spoon

knife

oven

serving plate

TROPICAL FRUIT MUFFINS

1 3/4 cups flour

1 Tablespoon sugar substitute*

2 teaspoons baking powder

1/4 teaspoon baking soda

1/2 teaspoon salt

1/4 cup coconut, shredded

3 ripe bananas

1/3 cup melted margarine

1 egg

1 teaspoon grated orange rind

1/3 cup orange juice

1. Mix together flour, sugar substitute, baking powder, baking soda, and salt.

2. Stir in coconut and make a well.

3. Combine bananas, margarine, egg, orange rind, and juice in small bowl.

4. Add to dry ingredients and stir until blended.

5. Spoon into greased muffin tins and fill 2/3 full.

6. Bake at 375°F for 20 minutes or until browned.

* Some sugar substitutes lose their sweetness when used in baking so check the package to be sure it can be used in baking.

EQUIPMENT NEEDED

2 bowls

measuring spoons

spatula

grater

knife

oven

serving plate

measuring cups

spoon

fork

waxed paper

muffin tins

non-stick spray

paper towels

ZUCCHINI BRAN MUFFINS

1/4 cup melted margarine

3/4 cup milk

1 egg

1 cup all bran cereal

3/4 cup shredded zucchini

1/4 teaspoon nutmeg

1 1/4 cups flour

1/3 cup sugar

4 teaspoons baking powder

1/2 teaspoon salt

1/2 teaspoon cinnamon

pinch of cloves

1. Whisk melted margarine, milk, and egg, add all bran cereal and let stand for 10 minutes. Add shredded zucchini.
2. Combine flour, sugar, baking powder, salt, cinnamon, and cloves in large bowl.
3. Stir liquid ingredients into dry ingredients until all are moistened.
4. Spoon into greased muffin tins.
5. Bake at 400°F for 15 to 20 minutes.

EQUIPMENT NEEDED

2 bowls

waxed paper

measuring spoons

spatula

non-stick spray

knife

paper towels

grater

measuring cups

2 spoons

muffin tins

oven

serving plate

ZUCCHINI MUFFINS

2 eggs

1 cup sugar

1/2 cup oil

2 teaspoons vanilla

1 cup shredded zucchini

1 1/2 cups flour

1/2 teaspoon salt

1/2 teaspoon baking powder

2 teaspoons cinnamon

1. Beat eggs until frothy in a large bowl.
2. Add sugar, oil, and vanilla and beat until well blended.
3. Add zucchini, flour, salt, baking powder, and cinnamon.
4. Mix until blended.
5. Spray muffin tins and spoon batter into muffin tins.
6. Bake at 350°F for 25 to 30 minutes or until browned.

EQUIPMENT NEEDED

bowl

measuring spoons

spatula

waxed paper

non-stick spray

knife

paper towels

measuring cups

spoon

grater

muffin tins

oven

serving plate

MAIN DISHES

ENGLISH MUFFIN OR BISCUIT PIZZA

Pizza sauce or 1 teaspoon oregano, 1 clove garlic, minced, 1 can tomato paste.

1 cup shredded cheese   1/4 cup grated Parmesan cheese

Packages of refrigerated biscuits or English muffins

1. Mix oregano, garlic, and tomato paste.
2. If biscuits, grease baking sheet, flatten biscuit to 4" circles with custard cup to leave a rim or split English muffins.
3. Add sauce, sprinkle with cheese.
4. Bake at 425°F for 10 minutes.

EQUIPMENT NEEDED

oven   foil or baking sheet

grater   knife

pancake turner   2 bowls

2 spoons   paper towels

non-stick spray

MUSHROOM QUICHE

pastry for 2 crust pie

1 medium onion, sliced

2 cups mushroom, sliced

2 Tablespoons margarine

1/2 cup milk

1/4 cup evaporated milk

1/4 teaspoon salt

pepper

3 Tablespoons flour

2 eggs

1. Cut pastry with circle cutter to fit mini-muffin tin cups.
2. Cook onion and mushrooms in margarine in sauce pan on hot plate.
3. Mix in flour and gradually add milk then bring to a boil.
4. Slowly add eggs, then the remaining ingredients.
5. Spoon into cups.
6. Bake at 350°F for 20-25 minutes.

EQUIPMENT NEEDED

mini-muffin tins

waxed paper

oven

bowl

measuring cups

spoon

knife

serving dish

cutter

rolling pin

hot plate

sauce pan

measuring spoons

spatula

paper towels

MUSHROOM PIZZA

1 can refrigerated crescent rolls

2 4 ounce cans mushroom or

    2 cups fresh mushroom slices

1/4 cup melted margarine

grated Parmesan cheese

1/4 teaspoon marjoram

1. Separate dough into triangles. Press enough triangles together to cover ungreased pan.
2. Toss margarine with mushrooms and arrange on dough.
3. Sprinkle with cheese and marjoram.
4. Bake at 375°F for 15 to 18 minutes.

EQUIPMENT NEEDED

can opener or knife

measuring cup

oven

paper towels

measuring spoons

baking sheet

serving dish

VEGETABLE PIZZA

SAUCE

1/3 cup pizza sauce

1/2 cup grated Parmesan cheese

1/2 cup thinly sliced onion

1/2 cup seeded plum tomatoes

1 cup shredded mozzarella cheese

1 green pepper, diced

1/2 cup mushrooms

1/2 cup broccoli bits

DOUGH RECIPE

1 package yeast

3/4 cup warm water

2 1/2 cup Bisquick

1 1/2 teaspoons oil

1. Soften yeast in warm water, add Bisquick and oil and beat for 2 minutes.
2. Dust waxed paper with biscuit mix and knead dough until smooth.
3. Divide dough in half and pat or shape on greased pan.
4. Proceed with sauce, veggies, and cheeses.
5. Bake at 425ºF for 5 to 10 minutes or until vegetables are tender.

EQUIPMENT NEEDED

oven

measuring cups

waxed paper

knife

grater

spatula

serving dish

2 bowls

measuring spoons

trays

cutting board

spoon

paper towels

non-stick spray

VEGETARIAN PIZZA

1/2 cup chopped onion

1 clove minced garlic

4 cups chopped tomatoes

3 Tablespoons red wine vinegar

2 teaspoons minced basil

2 teaspoons oregano

1/4 teaspoon pepper

3 whole wheat pita bread

1 cup shredded cheddar cheese

1 pepper, chopped

1 zucchini, thinly sliced

3 ounces sliced mushrooms

2 Tablespoons Parmesan cheese

1. Coat electric frying pan with spray and set for medium heat.
2. Add onion and garlic and sauté.
3. Add tomatoes, vinegar, basil, oregano, and pepper. Bring to a boil and simmer uncovered for 20 minutes, Remove from heat.
4. Cut pita carefully in half. Bake at 450°F for 5 minutes.
5. Spread 1/4 cup tomato sauce on each. Sprinkle with cheddar cheese and arrange vegetables on top of cheese and sprinkle with Parmesan cheese.
6. Bake at 450°F for 10 minutes or until cheese and veggies are tender.

EQUIPMENT NEEDED

electric frying pan

cutting board

measuring cups

wooden spoon

baking sheets

waxed paper

serving dish

non-stick spray

knife

measuring spoons

oven

grater

pancake turner

paper towels

ZUCCHINI QUESADILLAS

2 Tablespoons oil

1 onion, chopped

2 garlic cloves, minced

4 zucchini, shredded

1 green pepper, chopped

2 teaspoons chili powder

2 cups shredded Monterey Jack cheese

1 teaspoon cumin

1 teaspoon ground coriander

cayenne pepper

salt and pepper

1/4 cup salsa

8 flour tortillas

1. Heat oil in electric frying pan, sauté onion and garlic.
2. Add zucchini and bell pepper, cook until soft, stirring often.
3. Mix in seasonings and salsa. Place in bowl.
4. Heat greased frying pan to 375°F, place tortilla in pan, top with zucchini mixture, then cheese, cover with another tortilla. Cook in covered pan 10 minutes.
5. Serve immediately.

EQUIPMENT NEEDED

electric frying pan

measuring cups

bowl

spatula

pancake turner

non-stick spray

paper towels

measuring spoons

spoon

grater

knife

serving dish

cutting board

DESSERTS

ALMOND COOKIES

1/4 cup + 2 Tablespoons margarine

1 teaspoon sugar substitute*

1 egg yolk

1/2 teaspoon almond extract

1/8 teaspoon salt

1/4 teaspoon vanilla

1/4 teaspoon lemon extract

1 cup flour

1/2 teaspoon baking powder

1. Cream margarine and sugar substitute in medium bowl. Beat at medium speed until light and fluffy.
2. Add egg yolk and flavorings and beat well.
3. Combine flour, baking powder and salt and add to creamed mixture. Beat well.
4. Shape dough in 1" balls and place 2" apart on ungreased cookie sheet. Press each with a fork to flatten.
5. Bake at 300°F for 20 minutes or until edges begin to brown.
6. Remove cookies to wire racks to cool completely.

*Sugar substitute can lose its sweetness during baking. Be sure to check package to be sure it can be used in baking.

EQUIPMENT NEEDED

bowl

measuring spoons

spoon

baking sheets

oven

serving plate

measuring cups

electric mixer

spatula

fork

pancake turner

paper towels

ALMOND NUT CUPS

1 3 ounces cream cheese

1/2 cup margarine

1 cup flour

1/2 teaspoon vanilla

1/4 teaspoon salt

1/4 cup ground toasted almonds

1 egg

1 cup brown sugar

1 Tablespoon melted margarine

1 Tablespoon lemon juice or amaretto

1. Beat together cream cheese, margarine, flour, vanilla and salt in medium bowl.

2. Pat about 1 Tablespoon mixture into muffin tin making a depression to form crust.

3. Beat egg and combine with sugar. Add nuts, melted margarine, and lemon juice or amaretto.

4. Spoon into muffin tins.

5. Bake at 350°F for 30 minutes or until browned.

EQUIPMENT NEEDED

bowl

measuring spoons

spatula

muffin tins

serving plate

measuring cups

spoon

knife

oven

paper towels

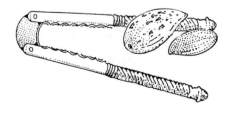

ANGEL SWEETS

1 cup chocolate chips

2 Tablespoons margarine

1 egg

1 cup confectioner's sugar

1 cup chopped nuts (optional)

2 cups mini marshmallows

1/2 cup flaked coconut

1. Melt the chocolate and margarine in sauce pan on a hot plate.
2. Remove from heat, blend in egg.
3. Stir in sugar, nuts and marshmallows and blend well or place in zip lock bag and pass around for mixing.
4. Shape into 1" balls and roll in coconut.

EQUIPMENT NEEDED

sauce pan

measuring cups

spoon

zip lock bags

serving plate

bowl

hot plate

measuring spoons

spatula

teaspoon

paper towels

APPLE CRISP

4 cups apple slices   1/2 cup brown sugar

2 Tablespoons lemon juice   1/4 cup margarine

1/2 cup flour   1 teaspoon cinnamon

1. Slice apples into baking dish and sprinkle with lemon juice.
2. Blend flour, brown sugar, margarine, and cinnamon and spread over apples.
3. Bake 30 minutes at 375° F.
4. Serve warm either plain or with milk.

EQUIPMENT NEEDED

baking dishes   bowl

knife   measuring cups

measuring spoons   cutting board

pastry blender   oven

APPLESAUCE

3 pounds apples	sugar
lemon juice	cinnamon
1 cup crushed pineapple	1 cup cranberry sauce

1. Wash and quarter apples. (If not using a food mill, core apples)
2. Cook partially covered with water. Use enough water to prevent apples burning.
3. Simmer until tender.
4. Put through food mill or sieve.
5. Return to saucepan, add sugar to taste.
6. Cook gently for 3 minutes.
7. Add lemon juice (if necessary) and cinnamon to taste.
8. Divide into thirds, add pineapple to 1/3, cranberry sauce to 1/3, and leave 1/3 plain.
9. Compare taste tests.

EQUIPMENT NEEDED

knife	saucepan
hot plate	wooden spoon
spatula	food mill or sieve
bowls	serving spoons

APRICOT ALMOND COFFEECAKE

1 cup toasted almonds

1/2 cup margarine

1/2 cup sugar

3 eggs

1 teaspoon lemon peel

1 Tablespoon lemon juice

1/2 teaspoon vanilla

1/2 cup flour

12 to 14 apricots, halved and pitted

3 Tablespoons packed brown sugar

1. Spread almonds in pan. Bake at 350°F until golden brown. Cool and finely grind in food processor or blender.

2. In large bowl, cream margarine and sugar until creamy.

3. Add eggs one at a time and beat well after each addition.

4. Beat in lemon peel, lemon juice, and vanilla.

5. Add flour and ground almonds and mix thoroughly.

6. Spray muffin tins with non-stick spray and flour.

7. Place batter in tins and arrange each with half (or less if large) apricot and sprinkle with brown sugar.

8. Bake at 375°F until batter is brown and center is firm when lightly pressed about 20 minutes.

9. Cool on rack and serve.

EQUIPMENT NEEDED

oven

bowl

spatula

measuring spoons

non-stick spray

serving plate

knife

food processor

spoon

measuring cups

mini muffin tins

racks

paper towels

BLUEBERRY BUCKLE

1/2 cup margarine	1/2 cup milk
3/4 cup sugar	2 cups blueberries
1 egg	1/2 cup sugar
2 cups flour	1/2 cup flour
2 1/2 teaspoons baking powder	1/2 teaspoon cinnamon
1/4 teaspoon salt	1/4 cup margarine

1. Cream margarine and 3/4 cup sugar in large bowl.
2. Add egg and beat until light and fluffy.
3. Add dry ingredients alternately with milk.
4. Place in greased cupcake tins.
5. Top with berries.
6. Mix crumbs of 1/2 cup sugar, 1/2 cup flour, and cinnamon.
7. Sprinkle over berries.
8. Bake at 350°F for 25 minutes, then cool on wire racks.
9. Serve warm.

EQUIPMENT NEEDED

2 bowls	2 cup measure
wooden spoon	non-stick spray
metal teaspoon	knife
measuring cups	wire racks
measuring spoons	paper towels
muffin tins	fork
serving tray	

BLUEBERRY ROLLS

2 cups flour

1 Tablespoon sugar

3 teaspoons baking powder

1/2 teaspoon salt

1/4 cup sugar

6 Tablespoons margarine

1 egg

2/3 cup milk

1 Tablespoon melted margarine

1/2 teaspoon cinnamon

1. Mix flour, 1 Tablespoon sugar, baking powder, and salt in large bowl.
2. Cut in margarine.
3. Mix egg and milk and add all at once. Stir until moistened.
4. Prepare blueberry filling:

   dash of salt

   1 Tablespoon lemon juice

   1 pint blueberries

   2 Tablespoons flour

   1/2 cup sugar

   a. Cook blueberries in small amount of water until tender and drain saving liquid.
   b. Use 1 cup of the liquid drained. Blend flour, sugar and salt and gradually add to the liquid. Cook until bubbly.
   c. Add lemon juice and pour into 9"x9" pan or pan to fit in oven.
5. Roll dough into 12"x8" rectangle and brush with melted margarine.
6. Sprinkle with 1/4 cup sugar and cinnamon mixed and top with blueberry filling.
7. Roll like jelly roll and seal.
8. Cut into 12 slices, place cut side down on top of sauce.
9. Bake at 450°F for 25 to 30 minutes.

EQUIPMENT NEEDED

2 bowls

measuring spoons

2 spoons

saucepan

hot plate

waxed paper

knife

paper towels

measuring cups

pastry blender

spatula

baking pan

strainer

rolling pin

serving plate

oven

BROWNIES

1 cup sugar	1/4 teaspoon salt
1/3 cup cocoa	3/4 cup flour
1/3 cup melted margarine	1/2 teaspoon baking powder
2 eggs	1 teaspoon vanilla

1. Combine sugar and cocoa in bowl. Add melted margarine.
2. Add unbeaten eggs.
3. Stir mixture into dry ingredients. Add vanilla.
4. Bake in greased pan 350°F for 25 minutes or until it starts to pull away from the edge of the pan.
5. Cut into squares and serve.

EQUIPMENT NEEDED

2 bowls	measuring cups
measuring spoons	spoon
spatula	pan
oven	non-stick spray
knife	serving plate
paper towels	

CARROT CAKE

1 1/2 cups flour	1/2 teaspoon salt
3/4 cup sugar	2/3 cup oil
1 teaspoon baking powder	2 eggs
1 teaspoon baking soda	1 cup shredded carrot
1 teaspoon cinnamon	1/2 cup crushed pineapple
1 teaspoon vanilla	1 cup raisins

1. Mix flour, sugar, baking powder, baking soda, cinnamon and salt in a bowl.
2. Add oil, eggs, carrots, crushed pineapple, raisins, and vanilla to dry ingredients and mix well.
3. Beat for two minutes.
4. Put into greased muffin tins and bake at 350°F for 15 to 20 minutes.
5. Cool cakes and ice with cream cheese icing.

CREAM CHEESE ICING

3 ounces cream cheese	2 cups confectioner's sugar
1 Tablespoon margarine	1 teaspoon vanilla

Beat ingredients until fluffy.

EQUIPMENT NEEDED

2 bowls	measuring cups
measuring spoons	2 spoons
spatula	grater
waxed paper	muffin tins
non-stick spray	oven
knife	wire racks
serving plate	paper towels

CARROT CAKE II

2 eggs

1/3 cup oil

1/3 cup honey

1 cup + 3 Tablespoons whole wheat flour

1 cup grated carrots

1 teaspoon cinnamon

1 teaspoon salt

1 1/4 teaspoon baking soda

1 cup raisins

1. Lightly beat eggs and add oil and honey until well blended in large bowl.
2. Combine wheat flour, cinnamon, salt, and baking powder in small bowl.
3. Add flour mixture to egg mixture and blend well.
4. Add carrots and raisins.
5. Pour into greased muffin tins and bake at 350°F for 20 to 25 minutes.
6. Cool on racks and ice with cream cheese icing.

CREAM CHEESE ICING

3 ounces cream cheese

2 to 4 Tablespoons honey

2 to 4 Tablespoons lemon juice

1. Cream cream cheese and add honey and lemon juice to taste.
2. Beat until desired consistency.

EQUIPMENT NEEDED

2 bowls

measuring spoons

spatula

waxed paper

non-stick spray

knife

serving plate

measuring cups

2 spoons

grater

muffin tins

oven

wire racks

paper towels

CHOCOLATE BUTTER COOKIES

1/2 cup sugar

3/4 cup margarine, softened

1 egg yolk

1 teaspoon vanilla

1 1/2 cups flour

1/4 cup cocoa

1. Heat oven to 375°F.
2. In large bowl, combine sugar, margarine, egg yolk, and vanilla.
3. Beat until light and fluffy (2-3 min.).
4. Gradually add flour and cocoa until well mixed (2-3 min).
5. Shape as desired with cookie press or roll into ball and flatten with fork
6. Place 1" apart on cookie sheet.
7. Bake for 7-9 minutes or until set.
8. Cool and serve.

EQUIPMENT NEEDED

oven

bowl

measuring cups

measuring spoons

spoon

spatula

cookie press

baking sheets

serving dishes

pancake turner

paper towels

CHOCOLATE CHIPPER CHAMPS

1 1/2 cups brown sugar

3/4 cup margarine

1 teaspoon vanilla

2 eggs

1 cup M&M's

1 teaspoon baking soda

1/2 teaspoon salt

2 1/4 cups flour

1. Preheat oven to 350°F and spray baking sheets with non-stick spray.
2. Mix sugar, margarine, vanilla and eggs in a large bowl until well blended.
3. Stir in remaining ingredients.
4. Drop dough by rounded tablespoonful about 3" apart on lightly greased baking sheet.*
5. Press 3 or 4 additional candies in each cookie if desired.
6. Bake 10 to 12 minutes or until lightly browned. Cool slightly.

* If using toaster oven, make cookies much smaller and put closer together.

EQUIPMENT NEEDED

bowl

measuring spoons

spatula

baking sheets

oven

serving plate

measuring cups

spoon

pancake turner

non-stick spray

tablespoon or teaspoon

paper towels

CHOCOLATE CRINKLES

1/2 cup margarine	2 cups flour
1 cup sugar	2 teaspoons baking powder
2 teaspoons vanilla	1/2 teaspoon salt
2 eggs	1/3 cup milk
2 squares chocolate, melted	confectioner's sugar

1. Cream margarine, sugar, and vanilla in large bowl.
2. Beat in eggs, then melted chocolate.
3. Add flour, baking powder, salt alternately with milk.
4. Form into 1" balls and roll in confectioner's sugar.
5. Place on greased baking sheet 2" to 3" apart.
6. Bake at 350°F for 15 minutes.
7. Cool slightly and remove from pan.

EQUIPMENT NEEDED

bowl	electric mixer
measuring cups	measuring spoons
spatula	pancake turner
waxed paper	baking sheets
oven	non-stick spray
serving plate	paper towels

CHOCOLATE CUPCAKES

1 cup flour

3/4 cup sugar

3/8 cup (3 Tbs.) cocoa

5/8 cup (5 Tbs.) milk

3/8 cup (3 Tbs.)shortening

1 egg

1 teaspoon baking soda

1/2 teaspoon salt

1/2 teaspoon vanilla

1/4 teaspoon baking powder

1. Preheat oven to 350° F.
2. In large bowl, measure all ingredients.
3. With mixer at low speed, beat until well mixed, then at high speed for five minutes.
4. Spoon into muffin tins that have been greased. Fill tins half full.
5. Bake for 20 minutes or until firm to the touch. Cool 10 minutes before icing.

CREAM CHEESE ICING

3 ounces cream cheese

1 1/2 Tablespoons milk

orange food coloring (Halloween)

1/2 teaspoon vanilla

3/4 cup confectioners' sugar

1. Cream cream cheese and milk.
2. Beat in confectioners' sugar and add more to make the right consistency.
3. Dip cupcake into icing and swirl then garnish.

EQUIPMENT NEEDED

2 bowls

measuring spoons

spatula

oven

serving plates

non-stick spray

measuring cups

mixer

muffin tins

spoon

paper towels

knife

CHOCOLATE CUT-OUTS

1 cup + 3 Tablespoons flour

3 Tablespoons cocoa

pinch of salt

1/2 cup unsalted butter

7/8 cup confectioners' sugar

1/2 square melted baking chocolate

1/2 teaspoon vanilla

1. Preheat oven to 325°F.
2. Combine flour, cocoa, and salt in small bowl.
3. Beat butter, add sugar, melted chocolate, and vanilla in bowl until light and fluffy.
4. Beat in dry ingredients until blended.
5. Knead dough until smooth.
6. Divide in half and roll each half between two pieces of waxed paper until 1/4"
   thick. Cut into desired shapes with cookie cutters.
7. Bake on ungreased baking sheet 10 to 12 minutes or until firm to touch. Cool.

EQUIPMENT NEEDED

2 bowls

measuring spoons

spatula

rolling pin

baking sheets

oven

serving plates

measuring cups

spoon

waxed paper

cookie cutters

pancake turner

paper towels

CHRISTMAS TREES

1 cup margarine

3/4 cup sugar

1 egg

1 teaspoon vanilla

2 1/4 cups flour

1/4 teaspoon baking powder

green sugar

1. Beat margarine and sugar until fluffy in a medium bowl.
2. Beat in egg and vanilla.
3. Add flour and baking powder and mix well.
4. Place dough in cookie press with tree plate and pack in firmly.
5. Force dough out on ungreased baking sheet.
6. Sprinkle with green sugar.
7. Bake at 375°F for 10 to 12 minutes.

EQUIPMENT NEEDED

bowl

measuring spoons

spatula

baking sheets

pancake turner

paper towels

measuring cups

spoon

cookie press

oven

serving plate

COFFEE CAKE

1 1/2 cups flour   1/4 to 1/2 cup sugar
1/4 teaspoon salt   1 egg
2 teaspoons baking powder   2/3 cup milk
1/4 cup margarine   1/2 teaspoon vanilla

1. Cream margarine and sugar in a large bowl.
2. Beat in egg.
3. Add flour, salt, and baking powder alternately with milk and vanilla.
4. Pour into greased pan 9" square or 2 smaller pans.
5. Top with pitted cherries or Streusel mixture.

STREUSEL MIXTURE

2 Tablespoons flour   2 Tablespoons margarine
5 Tablespoons sugar   1/2 teaspoon cinnamon

   Mix together and sprinkle on top of cake.

6. Bake at 375°F for 25 minutes or until it springs back to touch.

EQUIPMENT NEEDED

2 bowls   measuring cups
measuring spoons   2 spoons
spatula   knife
pan   non-stick spray
oven   serving plate
paper towels

CONGO SQUARES

2 2/3 cups flour

2 1/2 teaspoons baking powder

1/2 teaspoon salt

2/3 cup margarine

2 1/4 cups brown sugar

3 eggs

1 cup broken nuts (optional)

1 package chocolate chips (6 ounces)

1. Mix together flour, baking powder and salt in small bowl.
2. Melt margarine in saucepan.
3. Stir brown sugar into melted margarine and allow to cool slightly.
4. Beat eggs one at a time into sugar mixture.
5. Add flour mixture, nuts and chocolate chips.
6. Pour into waxed paper lined pan 15"x10"x1" or several smaller pans.
7. Bake at 350°F for 25 to 30 minutes or until browned.

EQUIPMENT NEEDED

hot plate

measuring cups

jelly roll pan or baking sheets

spoon

spatula

paper towels

saucepan

measuring spoons

waxed paper

knife

serving plate

small bowl

CREAM CHEESE COOKIES

2 3 ounce packages cream cheese   2 cups flour

1 cup margarine   jelly or jam

1. Cream cheese and margarine together in a medium bowl.
2. Add flour gradually and mix well.
3. Form into balls by teaspoonfuls.
4. Place on baking sheet and make deep well with thumb or spoon.
5. Bake at 425°F for 15 minutes.
6. Cool and fill depression with jelly or jam.
7. These cookie do not keep well filled. If storing, fill with jelly or jam on use.

EQUIPMENT NEEDED

bowl   measuring cup

spoon   spatula

baking sheet   oven

teaspoon   serving plate

paper towels

CUPCAKES WITH JELLY FROSTING

1/2 cup margarine	1/2 teaspoon salt
1 3/4 cups flour	1 egg
3/4 cup sugar	3/4 cup milk
2 teaspoons baking powder	1 teaspoon vanilla

1. Preheat oven to 375°F.
2. Place margarine in a bowl and mix until softened.
3. Add flour, sugar, baking powder, and salt.
4. Add egg and half the milk, mix until flour is moistened. Beat 2 minutes.
5. Add remaining milk and vanilla. Beat 1 minute.
6. Fill greased muffin tins 1/2 full.
7. Bake 18 to 20 minutes or until browned.
8. Cool and frost.

JELLY FROSTING

1/2 cup tart jelly	1 unbeaten egg white
2 Tablespoons sugar	dash of salt

1. Combine ingredients in top of double boiler and over boiling water.
2. Beat and cook until stiff peaks form.
3. Remove from heat and beat 2 minutes.
4. Frost cupcakes.

EQUIPMENT NEEDED

bowl	measuring cups
measuring spoons	spoon
spatula	muffin tins
non-stick spray	oven
hot plate	double boiler
electric mixer	spatula
knife	serving plate
paper towels	

DATE AND COCONUT BALLS

1/2 cup margarine

3/4 cup brown sugar

1 teaspoon vanilla

1 10 ounce package chopped dates

3 cups toasted rice cereal

1 7 ounce package flaked coconut

1. In saucepan, melt margarine over medium heat.
2. Sir in brown sugar and dates.
3. Cook stirring constantly until dates dissolve and mixture thickens.
4. Remove from heat and add cereal, vanilla and 1 cup coconut.
5. Cool and shape into 1' balls and roll in remaining coconut.
6. Place on waxed paper to cool.

EQUIPMENT NEEDED

hot plate

measuring cups

2 spoons

waxed paper

paper towels

saucepan

measuring spoons

spatula

serving plate

114

FRESH FRUIT TARTS

PIE CRUST

1 package of pie crust mix   water

1. Follow directions on package but place in ziplock freezer bag and pass around to have bag squeezed to mix crust.
2. Roll on floured waxed paper 1/4 inch thick and cut with round cookie cutter.
3. Place in mini muffin tins and prick with fork.
4. Bake at 450°F for 8 to 10 minutes.

FILLING

2 slightly beaten egg yolks   2 cup milk

1 3 ounce package regular vanilla pudding mix (not instant)

2 3 ounce packages cream cheese   2 egg whites

1/4 cup sugar   fruit (canned or soft fresh)

1. Combine beaten egg yolk and milk. Cook according to package directions with pudding. Remove from heat.
2. Cut cream cheese into bits and add to hot pudding. Allow to stand 10 minute. Mix well.
3. Beat egg white to soft peaks and add sugar. Continue beating until stiff. Fold into pudding.
4. Spoon into tart shells and spoon fruit over tarts.

EQUIPMENT NEEDED

bowl	rolling pin
circle cutter	fork
oven	muffin tins
flour	pan
hot plate	measuring cups
measuring spoons	electric mixer
spoon	serving plate
paper towels	waxed paper
freezer zip lock bag	

GERMAN APPLE CAKE

2 cups whole wheat flour

1 Tablespoon baking powder

1/2 teaspoon cinnamon

1/2 teaspoon nutmeg

1/4 cup margarine

thin apple slices from 1 apple

1 egg

1/2 cup milk

1/4 cup honey

1 teaspoon vanilla

1 cup finely chopped apples

1. Combine wheat flour, baking powder, cinnamon, and nutmeg.
2. Add margarine that is cut into chunks and work into dry ingredients with hands.
3. Mix liquid ingredients together and add to dry and mix well.
4. Add chopped apple and mix.
5. Pour into sprayed muffin tins. Add an apple slice on top.
6. Bake at 350°F for 20 minutes or until done. Serve warm with

APPLE BUTTER SWIRL TOPPING

1 cup cottage cheese

1 teaspoon vanilla

2 Tablespoons honey

3 Tablespoons apple butter

1. Smooth cottage cheese in blender. Add honey and vanilla.
2. In bowl, add apple butter and swirl to make a pretty pattern. Serve on top of cake.

EQUIPMENT NEEDED

oven

measuring cups

spoon

knife

serving dish

non-stick spray

2 bowls

measuring spoons

spatula

cutting board

paper towels

GUM DROP COOKIES

1/2 cup margarine

1 cup brown sugar

1 egg

1/4 cup water

1 3/4 cups flour

1/2 teaspoon baking soda

1/2 teaspoon salt

1 1/2 cups cut up gum drops

1. Cream margarine and sugar together in a large bowl.
2. Add egg and beat well.
3. Add flour, baking soda, and salt alternately with water.
4. Drop by teaspoon on a greased cookie sheet.
5. Bake for 10 minutes at 400°F.

EQUIPMENT NEEDED

oven

bowl

measuring spoons

spatula

knife

paper towels

baking sheets

measuring cups

2 spoons

pancake turner

non-stick spray

serving dish

(I use green spearment gum drops in this recipe for St. Patrick's Day.)

LIGHT BROWNIES

6 Tablespoons margarine	2 slightly beaten egg whites*
1 cup sugar	1/2 cup flour
1/2 cup cocoa	1/4 cup chopped nuts (optional)
1 teaspoon vanilla	powdered sugar

1. Preheat oven to 350°F and spray baking pan with non-stick spray.
2. Melt margarine, add sugar and stir until blended.
3. Stir in cocoa and vanilla.
4. Add egg whites and stir until blended.
5. Stir in flour and nuts.
6. Pour into prepared pan and bake 25 minutes or until edges pull away from sides of pan.
7. Cool, cut, and sprinkle with powdered sugar.

* 1/2 cup egg substitute can be used instead of egg whites.

EQUIPMENT NEEDED

bowl	measuring cup
measuring spoons	spoon
spatula	knife
baking pan	oven
non-stick spray	serving dish
paper towels	

MINI CHOCOLATE CHIP CUPCAKES

1 1/4 cups flour

1 1/4 teaspoons baking powder

dash of salt

1/2 cup margarine

3/4 cup sugar

1 teaspoon vanilla

2 eggs

1/2 cup milk

6 oz. mini chocolate chips

1. Preheat oven to 375°.
2. In small bowl, combine flour, baking powder, and salt.
3. In large bowl, beat margarine, sugar, and vanilla until creamy.
4. Add eggs and beat well.
5. Blend in dry ingredients alternately with milk. Stir in chocolate chips.
6. Spoon batter into greased mini cups and bake 15 to 20 minutes.
7. Cool and ice if desired.

EQUIPMENT NEEDED

3 bowls

measuring cups

spatula

oven

knife

paper towels

measuring spoons

2 spoons

mini muffin tins

spray

serving dish

BUTTER ICING

1/4 cup margarine

1/2 teaspoon vanilla

1 1/2 cups confectioners' sugar

2 Tablespoons milk

1. Cream margarine. gradually add sugar alternately with milk and vanilla.
2. Spread on cool cupcakes and decorate with a mini chocolate chip.

NECTARINE CAKE

3 pounds nectarines

1 3/4 cups flour

1/2 cup sugar

2 1/2 teaspoons baking powder

1 teaspoon vanilla

1/2 cup margarine

1/2 teaspoon salt

1 egg

3/4 cup milk

whipped cream

1. Place margarine in bowl and mix to soften. Add flour, sugar, baking powder, and salt.
2. Add egg and half of the milk and mix to moisten, then beat 2 minutes.
3. Add remaining milk and vanilla and beat 1 minute.
4. Slice nectarines into bottom of greased pan and add batter.
5. Bake at 375°F for 18 to 20 minutes or until done to touch.
6. Cut and serve with whipped cream.

EQUIPMENT NEEDED

2 bowls

measuring spoons

spatula

non-stick spray

oven

paper towels

measuring cups

2 spoons

muffin tins

knife

serving plate

OATMEAL COOKIES

1 1/4 cups margarine

1/2 cup brown sugar

1/2 cup sugar

1 egg

1 teaspoon vanilla

1 1/2 cups flour

1 teaspoon salt

1 teaspoon cinnamon

1 teaspoon nutmeg

3 cups oats

1 teaspoon baking soda

1 cup raisins

1. Preheat oven to 375°F.
2. Beat margarine and sugars together until light and fluffy in large bowl.
3. Beat in egg and vanilla.
4. Combine dry ingredients and add to mixture in bowl mixing well.
5. Stir in oats and raisins.
6. Drop by tablespoons full on ungreased baking sheet.
7. Bake 8 to 11 minutes depending on crispness desired.
8. Cool on rack.

EQUIPMENT NEEDED

bowl

measuring spoons

spatula

baking sheets

tablespoon

paper towels

measuring cups

spoon

pancake turner

oven

serving plate

ORANGE-MAPLE PECAN BARS

3 cups graham cracker crumbs   1/2 cup confectioner's sugar

3 Tablespoons frozen orange juice concentrate, thawed

2 Tablespoons maple syrup   2 Tablespoons melted margarine

3/4 cup chopped pecans   confectioner's sugar

1. Line 9"x12" pan with foil extending over the edge of pan.
2. Mix crumbs, sugar, juice, syrup, margarine, and 3/8 cup pecans in a bowl until blended.
3. Place mixture in pan and press into even layer. Press remaining nuts on top and dust with sugar.
4. Use foil ends to lift out of pan and cut into squares. Lift off of foil onto serving plate.

EQUIPMENT NEEDED

pan   foil

measuring cups   measuring spoons

ziplock bag (for mixing)   knife

cutting board   spoon

sifter   serving plate

paper towels

PEACH AND BLUEBERRY SHORTCAKE

2 cups flour

1/4 cup sugar

1 Tablespoon baking powder

1 teaspoon grated orange peel

1/4 teaspoon nutmeg

1/2 cup margarine

1 egg

3/4 cup milk

1. Combine dry ingredients and cut in margarine until it resembles coarse sand.
2. Add egg and 2/3 cup milk and mix with a fork until dough is all moist.
3. Pat dough into a ball and flatten to 1/2 inch thick and cut into 2 1/2 " rounds with cookie cutter.
4. Place on ungreased baking sheet. Brush tops with remaining milk and sprinkle with sugar.
5. Bake at 400°F for 15 minutes or until golden brown.
6. Cool and split and serve with;

PEACH AND BLUEBERRY MIXTURE

4 peaches

1 Tablespoon lemon juice

whipped cream

1 cup blueberries

confectioners' sugar

1. Peel, pit and dice peaches. Sprinkle with lemon juice and stir in blueberries.
2. Sweeten to taste with confectioners' sugar.
3. Spoon on top of a half of shortcake. Top with whipped cream if desired.

EQUIPMENT NEEDED

2 bowls

measuring spoons

fork

waxed paper

baking sheets

knife

spoon

paper towels

measuring cups

pastry blender

spatula

cookie cutter

oven

cutting board

serving plate

PEACH CAKE

1 cup flour

1 teaspoon baking powder

1/4 teaspoon salt

2 Tablespoons sugar

2 Tablespoons margarine

1 egg

1/2 teaspoon vanilla

milk

4 cups peaches, peeled and sliced

1 cup sugar

2 teaspoons cinnamon

3 Tablespoons melted margarine

1. Mix together flour, baking powder, salt, and sugar in large bowl.

2. Cut in margarine until coarse crumbs form.

3. In a measuring cup beat egg and vanilla, then add milk to make a 1/2 cup of mixture.

5. Combine with flour mixture to make a stiff dough.

6. Pat into a greased pan.

7. Cover top evenly with peaches and sprinkle with sugar, cinnamon, and margarine mixture.

8. Bake at 425°F for 25 minutes or until browned.

EQUIPMENT NEEDED

bowl

measuring spoons

spoon

knife

small bowl

non-stick spray

serving plate

measuring cups

pastry blender

spatula

baking pan

spoon

oven

paper towels

PEACH COBBLER

1 cup flour

2 Tablespoons sugar

1 1/2 teaspoon baking powder

1/4 teaspoon salt

1/4 cup margarine

1/4 cup milk

1 egg

1. Mix together flour, sugar, baking powder, and salt in a large bowl.
2. Cut in margarine until coarse crumbs form.
3. Combine milk and egg. Add and stir until moistened.

PEACH MIXTURE

1 1/2 Tablespoons cornstarch

1/4 teaspoon mace

1/2 cup brown sugar

1 Tablespoon margarine

1/2 cup water

4 cups peaches, peeled and sliced

1 Tablespoon lemon juice

4. Combine cornstarch, mace, brown sugar, and water in saucepan.
5. Cook until thickened. Add peaches, lemon juice, and margarine.
7. Cook until heated thoroughly and pour into pan.
9. Spoon batter from recipe above in 6 mounds on top of peaches.
10. Bake at 400°F for 20 to 25 minutes or until browned.*

* May be made in electric frying pan at 230°F.

EQUIPMENT NEEDED

bowl

measuring spoons

spatula

hot plate

pan or fry pan

paper towels

measuring cups

2 spoons

pastry blender

saucepan

oven

knife

PEACH CRISP

4 cups peaches

2 Tablespoons lemon juice

1/2 cup flour

light cream or half and half cream

1/2 cup brown sugar

1/4 cup margarine

1 teaspoon cinnamon

1. Slice and peel peaches and place in baking pan.
2. Sprinkle with lemon juice.
3. Mix remaining ingredients to form crumbs.
4. Spread crumbs over peaches.
5. Bake at 375°F for 30 minutes.
6. Serve warm with cream.

EQUIPMENT NEEDED

2 bowls

knife

measuring spoons

oven

2 spoons

baking pan

measuring cups

pastry blender

paper towels

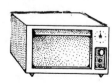

PEANUT BLOSSOMS

1 3/4 cups flour

1 teaspoon salt

1 teaspoon baking powder

1/2 cup margarine

1 teaspoon vanilla

1/2 cup peanut butter

1/2 cup sugar

1/2 cup brown sugar

1 egg

chocolate kisses

1. Cream margarine and peanut butter in a large bowl.
2. Add sugars and mix well.
3. Beat in egg and vanilla.
4. Blend in flour, salt, and baking powder.
5. Shape into balls and roll in sugar. Place on ungreased sheet.
6. Bake at 375°F for 8 minutes.
7. Remove from oven, press chocolate kiss in center of each ball hard enough to crack edges of cookie.
8. Return to oven for 2 to 5 minutes.

EQUIPMENT NEEDED

bowl

measuring spoons

spatula

baking sheet

serving plate

measuring cups

spoon

pancake turner

oven

paper towels

PEANUT BUTTER AND JELLY COOKIES

1 10 ounce bag peanut butter chips   2 Tablespoons regular margarine

2 Tablespoons peanut butter   3 Tablespoons jelly

3 1/2 cups sweetened oat and wheat bran cereal, finely crushed

1/4 cup unsalted roasted peanuts, chopped

1. Stir peanut butter chips, peanut butter, and margarine in a saucepan over very low heat until melted. Add cereal and stir until blended. Remove from heat.
2. Drop teaspoonfuls 2" apart on waxed paper. Press flat into 2" round and let stand for 20 minutes or until firm.
3. Spoon jelly into a cup and stir until liquid. Drizzle on cookies, then sprinkle with peanuts.

EQUIPMENT NEEDED

saucepan   hot plate

measuring cups   measuring spoons

2 spoons   spatula

waxed paper   ziplock freezer bag (to crush cereal)

serving plate   paper towels

PEANUT BUTTER COOKIES

1/2 cup unsalted margarine

1/2 cup sugar

1/2 cup brown sugar

1 egg

1 cup unsalted peanut butter

1/2 teaspoon vanilla

1 1/2 cups flour

1 1/4 teaspoon baking powder

1. Cream sugars with margarine in a large bowl.
2. Add peanut butter, egg, and vanilla.
3. Mix flour and baking powder together and add to other ingredients.
4. Form into 1 1/2" balls and place on greased cookie sheet 3" apart.
5. Press with fork and bake 350°F 10-15 minutes.

EQUIPMENT NEEDED

oven

measuring cups

spoon

baking sheets

pancake turner

paper towels

bowl

measuring spoons

spatula

non-stick spray

serving dish

PERSIMMON COOKIES

1/2 cup margarine

1 cup sugar

1 egg

1 teaspoon baking soda

1 cup persimmon pulp

2 cups flour

1/2 teaspoon cinnamon

1/2 teaspoon nutmeg

1/2 teaspoon cloves

1 cup pecans

1 cup chopped dates

1. Cream margarine and sugar in a large bowl.
2. Beat in egg.
3. Combine soda and persimmon and mix thoroughly, then add to batter.
4. Add flour, cinnamon, nutmeg, and cloves.
5. Mix in nuts and dates.
6. Bake 15 minutes on greased cookie sheet at 350°F.

EQUIPMENT NEEDED

bowl

measuring cups

spatula

cookie sheets

cutting board

paper towels

non-stick spray

spoon

measuring spoons

pancake turner

knife

oven

serving plate

PLUM AND NECTARINE CRISP

1 pound plums

1 pound nectarines

2 Tablespoons cornstarch

1/4 cup brown sugar

1/4 teaspoon cinnamon

1/2 cup oats

1/3 cup flour

1/4 teaspoon cinnamon

pinch of salt

5 Tablespoons margarine

1/3 cup brown sugar

1. Preheat oven to 375°F.
2. Pit and slice fruit, then mix with cornstarch, 1/4 cup brown sugar, and cinnamon with 1/4 cup water and cook for 5 minutes or until bubbly.
3. Transfer to baking pan.
4. Combine oats, 1/3 cup brown sugar, flour, cinnamon, and salt.
5. Add butter and cut into coarse crumbs.
6. Sprinkle over fruit.
7. Bake about 20 minutes.

EQUIPMENT NEEDED

knife

saucepan

measuring cups

spoon

pastry blender

oven

paper towels

cutting board

hot plate

measuring spoons

spatula

bowl

serving spoon

PLUM COFFEE CAKE

1 cup flour

1/2 cup sugar

1 teaspoon baking powder

1/4 teaspoon ground nutmeg

1/4 teaspoon ground cinnamon

2 large eggs

1/3 cup milk

3 Tablespoons melted margarine

5 firm-ripe plums,halved,pitted

1/2 teaspoon ground cinnamon plus

2 Tablespoons sugar

1. In large bowl, stir together flour, sugar, baking powder, nutmeg, and cinnamon.
2. In small bowl, stir together eggs, milk, and butter.
3. Add egg mixture to flour mixture and combine well.
4. Place batter in greased muffin tins.
5. Place plum pieces in center of each cupcake and press into batter slightly.
6. Sprinkle top of each cake with cinnamon and sugar.
7. Bake at 375°F for 20 to 25 minutes or until done.
8. Serve warm or cool. (Leftovers can be stored in refrigerator for up to 2 days.)

EQUIPMENT NEEDED

2 bowls (1 large and 1 small)

measuring cups

measuring spoons

custard cup

wooden spoon

rubber spatula

knife

muffin tins

non-stick spray

oven

serving dish

paper towels

STRAWBERRY SHORTCAKE

2 cups flour

2 Tablespoons sugar

3 teaspoons baking powder

1/2 teaspoon salt

whipped cream

1/2 cup margarine

1 egg

2/3 cup light cream

strawberries, sliced

1. Mix dry ingredients and cut in margarine until it resembles coarse crumbs in a large bowl.
2. Combine egg and light cream, then add all at once and stir until moist.
3. Knead gently on floured waxed paper for 1/2 minute.
4. Pat 1/2 inch thick.
5. Cut into biscuits.
6. Place on ungreased baking sheet and bake at 450°F for 10 minutes.
7. Split biscuit and add fruit, top with whipped cream.

EQUIPMENT NEEDED

oven

3 bowls

measuring spoons

spatula

knife

waxed paper

pastry blender

baking sheets

measuring cups

spoon

pancake turner

cookie cutter

paper towels

STRAWBERRY TARTLETS

PIE CRUST

1 package pie crust mix   water

1. Follow directions on package but place in ziplock freezer bag and pass around to have bag squeezed to mix crust.
2. Roll on floured waxed paper 1/8" thick and cut with round cookie cutter.
3. Place in mini-muffin tins and prick with fork.
4. Bake at 450°F for 8 to 10 minutes.

STRAWBERRY FILLING

1 pint strawberries   1/3 cup sugar

1 Tablespoon lemon juice   1 Tablespoon cornstarch

whipped cream

1. Clean, cut and mash berries in saucepan.
2. Add remaining ingredients and cook while stirring over low heat until thick and transparent.
3. Cool slightly. Place in tartlets and top with whipped cream.

EQUIPMENT NEEDED

oven	hot plate
ziplock bag	measuring spoons
rolling pin	waxed paper
flour	cookie cutter
fork	saucepan
1/3 cup measure	spoon
masher	mini-muffin tins
serving plate	paper towels

SUGAR COOKIES

3/8 cup margarine

1/2 cup sugar

1 egg

1/2 teaspoon vanilla

1/2 teaspoon lemon rind

1 1/2 cups flour

dash of salt

1. Beat margarine until soft in a large bowl.
2. Add sugar gradually and beat well.
3. Beat in egg and vanilla
4. Stir in flour, and salt gradually.
5. Roll dough very thin and cut into desired shape and place on greased cookie sheet.
6. Decorate and bake 8 minutes at 400°F.

EQUIPMENT NEEDED

bowl

measuring spoons

spatula

board

cookie sheets

serving dish

non-stick spray

measuring cups

spoon

rolling pin

cookie cutters

pancake turner

paper towels

SUGARLESS OATMEAL COOKIES

3 bananas, mashed

2 cups oats

1/2 cup raisins

1/3 cup margarine, melted

1/4 cup milk

1 teaspoon vanilla

1. Combine all ingredients, beating well in a large bowl. Let stand 5 minutes so oats can absorb moisture.
2. Drop dough by heaping teaspoons onto ungreased baking sheet.
3. Bake at 350°F for 15 to 20 minutes or until firm.
4. Let remain on cookie sheet 1 minute then transfer to racks to cool completely.

EQUIPMENT NEEDED

bowl

measuring spoons

spatula

baking sheets

racks

paper towels

measuring cups

spoon

teaspoon

oven

serving plate

SUNSHINE ORANGE CUPCAKES

1/3 cup margarine, melted

1/4 cup brown sugar substitute*

1 Tablespoon powdered sugar
    substitute*

1 egg

1 1/4 cups flour

2 teaspoons baking powder

1/2 teaspoon baking soda

1/4 teaspoon cinnamon

1/3 cup raisins

2/3 cup orange juice

1. Combine margarine, sugar substitutes, and egg in a medium size bowl. Beat
    2 minutes.
2. Combine flour, baking powder, baking soda,and cinnamon and stir in raisins.
3. Add flour mixture to creamed mixture alternately with orange juice.
4. Spoon into cupcake tins coated with baking spray.
5. Bake at 350°F for 15 to 20 minutes.

* Some sugar substitutes lose their sweetness in baking. Be sure to read label.

EQUIPMENT NEEDED

2 bowls

measuring spoons

rubber spatula

oven

knife

non-stick spray

measuring cups

wooden spoon

mini cupcake tins

paper towels

serving dish

INDEX

INDEX

INDEX